ELIJAH

A Man of Heroism and Humility

Publications by Charles R. Swindoll

BOOKS

Active Spirituality

The Bride

Compassion: Showing We Care
    in a Careless World

David: A Man of Passion
    and Destiny

Dear Graduate

Dropping Your Guard

Encourage Me

Esther: A Woman of Strength
    and Dignity

The Finishing Touch

Flying Closer to the Flame

For Those Who Hurt

God's Provision

The Grace Awakening

Growing Deep in the Christian Life

Growing Strong in the Seasons of Life

Growing Wise in Family Life

Hand Me Another Brick

Home: Where Life Makes Up Its Mind

Hope Again

Improving Your Serve

Intimacy with the Almighty

Joseph: A Man of Integrity
    and Forgiveness

Killing Giants, Pulling Thorns

Laugh Again

Leadership: Influence That Inspires

Living Above the Level of Mediocrity

Living Beyond the Daily Grind,
    Books I and II

The Living Insights Study Bible—
    General Editor

Living on the Ragged Edge

Make Up Your Mind

Man to Man

Moses: A Man of Selfless Dedication

The Mystery of God's Will

Paw Paw Chuck's Big Ideas in the
    Bible

The Quest for Character

Recovery: When Healing Takes Time

The Road to Armageddon

Sanctity of Life

Simple Faith

Simple Trust

Starting Over

Start Where You Are

Strengthening Your Grip

Stress Fractures

Strike the Original Match

The Strong Family

Suddenly One Morning

Tale of the Tardy Oxcart

Three Steps Forward, Two Steps Back

Victory: A Winning Game Plan for Life

You and Your Child

MINIBOOKS

BOOKLETS

A Man of Heroism and Humility

ELIJAH

Profiles in Character from

CHARLES R. SWINDOLL

WORD PUBLISHING

NASHVILLE

A Thomas Nelson Company

DEDICATION

Ever since I began my writing career back in 1975,
I have sought to dedicate each of my books to the person
who best fits its theme.
It is appropriate, therefore,
that I dedicate this volume to one who was
a magnificent model of the things I write about here:
the late, great

THOMAS WADE LANDRY

1924–2000

This outstanding Christian gentleman
was not only a world class player and coach in the game of football,
he was also a member of our Board of Incorporate Members at
Dallas Theological Seminary for twenty-three years,
my long-time friend,
and one of my own esteemed personal heroes.
I speak for the world at large when I say that
this was a better place when he walked among us.

We shall all miss his sterling example of quiet heroism and humility.

CONTENTS

INTRODUCTION

Elijah: A Man of Heroism and Humility

With a vivid memory of the military in my past, I find myself drawn to those who perform well under the pressure of battle. And some battles interest me more than others. For some reason, throughout my adult life, I have been especially intrigued with the American leaders who stood strong during our nation's saddest and bloodiest conflict—the infamous War Between the States. It is difficult to imagine the enormity of the tension that must have tormented the hearts of those brave soldiers and statesmen who, while engaged in warfare, realized the enemy was none other than a fellow American . . . sometimes a once-close friend or even a family member.

Among the many I have studied from that era of our history, no soldier stands taller than Robert E. Lee, a marvel of unimpeachable character and, to this day, of universal admiration. The mere mention of his name brings the term "gentleman" to mind. The virtues and vices of Lee's contemporaries, North and South—Davis, Longstreet, Grant, Scott, Pendleton, Sherman, Stuart, McClellan, Hood, and even Lincoln—remain debatable subjects. Not so with Lee. Somehow he has escaped such carping and criticism. In the minds of serious Civil War students, he remains a magnificent model of at least two character qualities rarely blended in one body, especially that of a strong leader: heroism and humility. Though tough at heart, the man remained tender of soul.

In his fine volume, *Call of Duty: The Sterling Nobility of Robert E. Lee*, J. Steven Wilkins captures a snapshot of those contrasting traits in the heat of a battle at Petersburg, where

> Lee found himself in an exposed position under intense fire. He ordered the men around him to seek shelter, and then stepped out into the open to pick up a baby sparrow that had fallen from a tree. Returning the sparrow to its nest, Lee followed his men to shelter.[1]

Never a general to hide safely far back behind the front lines, Lee frequently courted danger with an unflappable spirit of invincibility. He did his duty—and so much more—in the face of fear. Quietly confident, he conducted his life securely under the providential hand of God, in whom he trusted with a whole heart. While he never ran from the call to fight for what he truly believed to be the right, he was never one to call attention to himself, to enjoy the pomp and prestige of his rank or position, or to seek the applause of his admirers.

As I scan the dawn of this twenty-first century, I find myself asking, "Where is that kind of leader today?" Uncompromisingly strong, yet self-controlled. Disciplined, yet forgiving. Audaciously courageous, yet kind. Heroic in the heat of battle, yet humble in the aftermath. There are a few such men and women, admittedly, but therein lies the disappointment: The list is tragically short. One of my great hopes in my later years of life is to encourage more people to join the thin ranks of Lee-like leaders.

That, as much as anything, has prompted me to pick up my pen and return to another biblical character in the Great Lives from God's Word biographical series. I can think of few others who model these two invaluable traits more obviously than the prophet Elijah, whose calling was anything but calm and free from conflict. Nevertheless, as we are about to discover, the man exemplified true heroism and genuine humility amid the relentless pressure of battle.

Before we begin, however, let me pause here and express my gratitutde to those who played significant roles in my seeing this volume to completion. While the research and actual writing of the book were my own, I am indebted to three others who took my work with words and gave it wings to fly beyond the walls of my study. First, my careful and keen-eyed editor, Judith Markham, followed by Mary Hollingsworth, who greatly assisted me in finalizing the manuscript for publication, and Julie Meredith, who helped in securing the rights and permissions for the footnotes. These diligent and competent women deserve a lengthy standing ovation.

I also have two longtime publishing friends to thank: Joey Paul and Lee Gessner of Word Publishing. These two men, more than anyone else I could name, remained sources of determined, confident, and encouraging strength to me as the project fought for survival. Joey's willingness to adjust his schedule, based on my never-ending world of demands, added needed grace to an otherwise oppressive project and brought me great relief. It is a pleasure to publish with an organization staffed by such gracious gentlemen.

Finally, I want to acknowledge the behind-the-scenes support of several groups of close friends and family members who pray for me and believe in me. I'm referring to the faculty, staff, executive leadership team, and the Board of Incorporate Members at Dallas Theological Seminary . . . our board of directors and staff at Insight for Living . . . the elders, deacons, deaconesses, staff, fellow pastors, and congregation of our newly formed Stonebriar Community Church in Frisco, Texas . . . and my own family (including ten fabulous grandchildren!), and especially my wife of forty-five years, Cynthia. There is no way—*there is no way*—I could sustain my schedule (and maintain my sanity!) without the consistent intercessory support of these dear people to whom I am accountable and with whom I enjoy a relationship of harmony, loyalty, and love.

All the above-mentioned people join me in the hope that God will use my thoughts on the life of *Elijah: A Man of Heroism and Humility* to establish deep within you a desire to stand strong for what is right as you bow low before Him who is worthy of your trust and obedience. In a world that has lost its way, due in part to the lack of balanced, godly leadership, we are more than ever in need of a few Elijah-like men and women who are not afraid to live courageously before their peers as they walk humbly with their God.

—CHUCK SWINDOLL
Dallas, Texas

A Man of Heroism and Humility

ELIJAH

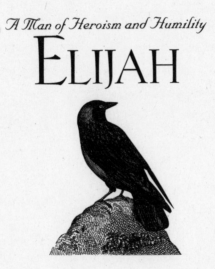

Now Ahab the son of Omri became king over Israel in the thirty-eighth year of Asa king of Judah, and Ahab the son of Omri reigned over Israel in Samaria twenty-two years. And Ahab the son of Omri did evil in the sight of the LORD more than all who were before him. And it came about, as though it had been a trivial thing for him to walk in the sins of Jeroboam the son of Nebat, that he married Jezebel the daughter of Ethbaal king of the Sidonians, and went to serve Baal and worshiped him. So he erected an altar for Baal in the house of Baal, which he built in Samaria. And Ahab also made the Asherah. Thus Ahab did more to provoke the LORD God of Israel than all the kings of Israel who were before him.

1 KINGS 16:29–33

Now Elijah the Tishbite, who was of the settlers of Gilead, said to Ahab, "As the LORD, the God of Israel lives, before whom I stand, surely there shall be neither dew nor rain these years, except by my word."

1 KINGS 17:1

CHAPTER ONE

Standing Alone in the Gap

A humble hero died on Saturday night, February 12, 2000. Born in Mission, Texas, in 1924, Thomas Wade Landry cast an unforgettable shadow along this earth's landscape for seventy-five years. What a remarkable blend of diligence, creativity, and strength in leadership he was. What a dynamic mix of dignity, discipline, and quiet confidence. What a class act! More importantly, what a legacy he left!

Like most famous heroes, Tom Landry lived his life in the public spotlight. His work was forever on display in an arena few in their right mind would choose: a dog-eat-dog world of competition, where privacy is invaded and criticism is constant. I'm referring, of course, to the high-powered and enormously pressurized National Football League, where head coaches are not known for their long-term tenure with any team. To borrow a line from one of the more colorful NFL coaches of the past, Coach Bum Phillips, "There's only two kinds of coaches—them that's been fired, and them that's gonna be." In today's win-no-matter-what world, coaches don't last.

But Coach Tom Landry did. For twenty-nine consecutive years he coached one team, the Dallas Cowboys, leaving such an indelible mark on his players that they still scramble to find the right words to describe their profound feelings of appreciation. His twenty consecutive winning seasons with the same team form a record in the ranks of professional football that will likely never be broken. Not anymore. Coaches aren't allowed to stay long enough to prove themselves winners. Greed, self-centered hype, and the public's insatiable hunger for immediate gratification undermine the patience that is needed to cultivate character on a team. But, thankfully, in Landry's era, he was allowed the time he needed to mentor his men, inspire them to great accomplishments, and best of all, impact their lives for lasting good. Small wonder he has become a legend.

It was my privilege to know Tom Landry up close and personal. He served on our Board of Incorporate Members at Dallas Theological Seminary for twenty-three years. Faithfully, he sat with us during some of our best years, as well as through some extremely difficult times. In the midst of both, he never failed to bring quiet-spoken wisdom and seasoned maturity to the table, adding perspective to our discussions and depth to our decisions.

Many heroes look better from a distance. Up close, however, they sometimes surprise and disappoint us. Not so with Tom Landry. The better you knew him, the more you admired him.

The world viewed Tom Landry from a distance and considered him a good man. I can tell you from experience, up close and personal, he was a great man. Great in integrity. Great in generosity. Great in determination. Great in priorities. (He referred to them often: God first, family second, football third.) Great in humility. When Tom Landry died, it seemed like the end of an era. The ranks of humble heroes are getting dangerously thin. Ours is fast becoming a world of self-important people who wear their successes much too conspicuously—whose achievements, rather than left unannounced for others to discover, are now shamelessly trumpeted by the achievers themselves.

I can't speak for everyone, but I think I do represent a majority when I say that we long to find authentic heroes who, when examined closely, are actually better than we expected. Our longing is even more greatly satisfied when we discover that these heroes have remained genuinely humble of heart. Such unique individuals stand alone in the gap. Nothing moves them. They are not intimidated by the opposition they face. They are not afraid of the challenges that loom before them. And they are not enamored of the press clippings that follow their accomplishments.

Exit, Head Coach Thomas Wade Landry.

Enter, Hebrew prophet Elijah.

We're first introduced to him as "Elijah the Tishbite" (1 Kings 17:1). Talk about stepping out of nowhere! If you think Landry's birthplace of Mission, Texas, seems like some remote, dusty town in the Lone Star State, try to locate Tishbeh in the ancient Middle Eastern land of Gilead. A scholar as reliable as the late Merrill F. Unger doesn't hesitate to emphasize the obscurity of the man's roots: "The term Tishbite refers to a native of a certain town by the name of Tishbeh, or something similar . . . a site of this name is unknown."[1]

I have a good friend who was reared so far out in the country, he says with a smile, "When I was a little boy, you had to go *toward town* to hunt." Sounds like Tishbeh! We can locate Gilead, but the town of Tishbeh—"or something similar"—is one of those places that the sands of time have completely hidden. Yet Elijah came out of this insignificant place—out of nowhere—to make such a significant contribution to God's plan for His people that he became one of Israel's most famous heroes. He became a legend.

But I'm getting ahead of myself. Let's back up and draw a deep breath of historical air so we can appreciate what this "great life from God's Word" meant to a forgotten and forlorn place in time.

THE CRUCIBLE OF HISTORY

When you study the lives of individuals, you must also study history. This is particularly true when we study the men and women whose accomplishments have stood the test of time and are now recorded in the annals as *significant* or *noteworthy*. You cannot separate people from the context of their times, because the steel of inner character is hammered out on the anvil of time and forged in the context of history. All great men or women experienced the heat of this refining fire, whether they were soldiers like

Robert E. Lee, poets like John Milton, statesmen like Alexander Solzhenitsyn, or rulers like Queen Esther.

In few lives are the hammer of history and the heat of the fire more evident than in the subject of this book. For that reason, it is vital that we understand the difficult times during which Elijah came on the biblical scene. Once we see the context of his life, we can begin to appreciate the strength of this unique, leathery figure, so ruggedly shaped by God to meet the rigors of his day.

The importance of context was brought home to me vividly years ago when our children were young, and our family was camping in Vermont. It was autumn, and the mountains were blanketed in red and yellow and orange. My oldest daughter, who was about four years old at the time, came running up to me with a fistful of wildflowers. "Look, Daddy," she said eagerly, "aren't they pretty?" I remember looking down at her scraggly little bouquet and saying with a smile, "Honey, show me where you got those flowers."

She ran ahead, drawing me toward a spot quite a distance from our campsite, and pointed to a patch of color amid weeds and thorns and jagged rocks. Nearby a few hornets were buzzing around a hole in a tree. To my shock, not more than three feet from the flowers was a ledge that dropped off about fifty or sixty feet, straight down.

Here, in rugged and dangerous surroundings, these little blossoms had grown unappreciated, unseen, unknown, until the eyes of a small girl (who had wandered much too far from camp!) had lighted on them. Once I saw the surroundings from which they had emerged, I appreciated that little fistful of flowers all the more.

Most of God's *greats* are like that. Elijah is certainly like that, which explains why I want to spend some time looking at the place from which this prophet out of nowhere emerged—this prophet who blossomed amid dangerous ledges and weeds of wickedness.

LET'S LEARN A LITTLE HISTORY

For well over a hundred years the Israelites had lived under the reign of three kings: Saul, then David, and finally Solomon. These three rulers of the Jews were great and famous men in many ways, although not one of them was without sin and failure. Then, at the end of King Solomon's life, a civil war broke out in the kingdom that had been united under God's anointed leadership. As strife grew in intensity, the nation became divided into a northern kingdom, most often called Israel, and a southern kingdom, usually referred to as Judah. This division remained until both kingdoms fell to foreign invaders, and the Jews were led away into captivity.

From the beginning of that division until Israel's captivity, a period of over two hundred years, the northern kingdom had nineteen monarchs, and all of them were wicked. Imagine that! Nineteen national leaders in succession, nineteen kings ruling back to back, who "did evil in the eyes of the Lord." That environment of evil prevailed in Israel until the Assyrians invaded in 722 B.C.

The southern kingdom, on the other hand, was under the leadership of seventeen rulers for well over three hundred years. Eight of these monarchs "followed the Lord their God," but nine of them were wicked men who did not serve or walk with God. The southern kingdom of Judah ended with the destruction of Jerusalem in 586 B.C. and the subsequent seventy-year Babylonian captivity. The southern kingdom was later revived when men such as Nehemiah, Ezra, and Zerubbabel returned from exile. They moved back into the land of their forefathers, rebuilt the temple, and restored the worship of the one true God.

If you have never done an in-depth study of this period of history, let me pause here and urge you to do so. I know how much this knowledge of Jewish history has helped me. I remember trying to read the Bible through when I was young. Things would go well until I came to the Book of First Kings. Invariably, when I reached that point I became confused. The names were tough enough, but with more than one king seemingly ruling at the same time, I would think, *This doesn't make sense.* The main problem was, I didn't understand the difference between Israel and Judah. But once I pieced together the history and harmonized it within the context of the various monarchs who ruled during a divided-kingdom era, this section of the Old Testament not only began to make sense but also came alive for me.

During this period of the northern and southern kingdoms, because of the wickedness of many of the kings and the apostasy of the Hebrew people, God sent various prophets to call both the rulers and the people to repentance. Being a prophet wasn't an easy calling. Most of the monarchs wanted nothing to do with God's anointed messengers, disdaining their warnings and ignoring their rebukes, or worse.

Let's look, for example, at Jeroboam, the first king over the northern kingdom. He is significant not only for his position as the first monarch of that era but also because he was the king who deliberately planted the seeds of idolatry among the people of Israel.

> After this event Jeroboam did not return from his evil way, but again he made priests of the high places from among all the people; any who would, he ordained, to be priests of the high places.
>
> 1 Kings 13:33

The term "high places" generally refers to pagan altars used for the worship of pagan gods and idols. So, right out of the chute, we learn that the first king of the northern kingdom ordained priests for the worship of false gods. Boldly and unashamedly, King Jeroboam promoted idolatry. Furthermore, he reigned for twenty-two years as a man of deception and murder. The northern kingdom was off to a tragic start with Jeroboam. And then came his son and successor, Nadab, who "reigned in his place."

> And the time that Jeroboam reigned was twenty-two years; and he slept with his fathers, and Nadab his son reigned in his place. . . . Now Nadab the son of Jeroboam became king over Israel in the second year of Asa king of Judah, and he reigned over Israel two years.
>
> 1 Kings 14:20; 15:25

Did you catch that? "Nadab—became *king over Israel* in *the second year of Asa king of Judah.*" See how that hint I mentioned helps you? One reigned over Israel, the other over Judah. Once you understand about the two separate kingdoms, you can see that Asa was ruling in the southern kingdom,

Judah, while Nadab was ruling in the northern kingdom, Israel. And what kind of king was Nadab?

> . . . he did evil in the sight of the LORD, and walked in the way of his father and in his sin which he made Israel sin.
>
> 1 Kings 15:26

But Nadab only lasted two years before he was assassinated by his successor.

> Then Baasha the son of Ahijah of the house of Issachar conspired against him, and Baasha struck him down at Gibbethon, which belonged to the Philistines, while Nadab and all Israel were laying siege to Gibbethon.
>
> So Baasha killed him in the third year of Asa king of Judah, and reigned in his place.
>
> 1 Kings 15:27–28

And what kind of a monarch was Baasha?

> And it came about, as soon as he was king, he struck down all the household of Jeroboam. He did not leave to Jeroboam any persons alive, until he had destroyed them, according to the word of the LORD, which He spoke by His servant Ahijah the Shilonite, and because of the sins of Jeroboam which he sinned, and which he made Israel sin, because of his provocation with which he provoked the LORD God of Israel to anger.
>
> 1 Kings 15:29–30

As I said, *all* of the northern rulers were bad, and some were worse than others. Baasha was not the worst, but he was definitely not the kind of guy you'd want your daughter to bring home! He was a wicked, murderous man, and he ruled Israel for twenty-four years. And then?

> Moreover, the word of the LORD through the prophet Jehu the son of Hanani also came against Baasha and his household, both because of

all the evil which he did in the sight of the LORD, provoking Him to anger with the work of his hands, in being like the house of Jeroboam, and because he struck it. In the twenty-sixth year of Asa king of Judah, Elah the son of Baasha became king over Israel at Tirzah, and reigned two years.

1 Kings 16:7–8

So once again we have a new king, Elah, on the throne of the northern kingdom. And what kind of a man was Elah? (I know this may seem monotonous, but bear with me—because all this sets the stage for Elijah's ministry.)

And his servant Zimri, commander of half his chariots, conspired against him. Now he was at Tirzah drinking himself drunk in the house of Arza, who was over the household at Tirzah.

Then Zimri went in and struck him and put him to death, in the twenty-seventh year of Asa king of Judah, and became king in his place.

And it came about, when he became king, as soon as he sat on his throne, that he killed all the household of Baasha; he did not leave a single male, neither of his relatives nor of his friends.

Thus Zimri destroyed all the household of Baasha, according to the word of the LORD, which He spoke against Baasha through Jehu the prophet, for all the sins of Baasha and the sins of Elah his son, which they sinned and which they made Israel sin, provoking the LORD God of Israel to anger with their idols.

1 Kings 16:9–13

Now wasn't that a dynasty? One murderer giving way to another murderer. One assassin killing another assassin. One mass murderer killing off the household of another mass murderer. A line of godless men coming to the throne and incessantly doing evil in the sight of the Lord.

Yet, as bad as that sounds, look at what the record says about Omri:

Then the people of Israel were divided into two parts: half of the people followed Tibni the son of Ginath, to make him king; the other half followed Omri.

But the people who followed Omri prevailed over the people who followed Tibni the son of Ginath. And Tibni died and Omri became king.

In the thirty-first year of Asa king of Judah, Omri became king over Israel, and reigned twelve years; he reigned six years at Tirzah.

And he bought the hill Samaria from Shemer for two talents of silver; and he built on the hill, and named the city which he built Samaria, after the name of Shemer, the owner of the hill.

And Omri *did evil in the sight of the LORD, and acted more wickedly than all who were before him.*

For he walked in all the way of Jeroboam the son of Nebat and in his sins which he made Israel sin, provoking the LORD God of Israel with their idols.

So Omri slept with his fathers, and was buried in Samaria; and Ahab his son became king in his place.

1 Kings 16:21–26, 28 (italics added)

Despite all the bloodshed and idolatry and wickedness of these previous kings, the writer still says that Omri "acted *more wickedly than all* who were before him." And then came his son Ahab!

Bloodshed and assassinations, murder and malice, intrigue and immorality, conspiracy and deception, hatred and idolatry had prevailed for six uninterrupted, dark decades in Israel. This reign of evil began in the heart of the one on the throne, and poured down into the very core of the people of the land. And then, of all things, they turned the throne over to Ahab, who married Jezebel, which is a little bit like going from Jesse James to Bonnie and Clyde.

AHAB AND JEZEBEL

At this point in 1 Kings, the historical narrative states that there was a marriage, and Jezebel is introduced.

And it came about, as though it had been a trivial thing for him to walk in the sins of Jeroboam the son of Nebat, that he married Jezebel the daughter of Ethbaal king of the Sidonians, and went to serve Baal and worshiped him.

1 Kings 16:31

Without even knowing what will follow, this offers a clue to this woman's significance in the history of Israel, because in the previous chronicles of the history of the northern kingdom we are never told the names of the wives of the kings. Now, suddenly, we are not only given the name of the next king, Ahab, but are also given the name of the woman he married. Jezebel.

Why? Why does God have the writer pause at this point and linger over the marriage of a monarch? Why make a point of telling us the name and lineage of Ahab's wife? I believe there are two primary reasons.

First, she was the dominant partner in the marriage. Jezebel really ruled the kingdom. She was the power behind the throne. Ahab's administration was, in every sense of the word, a *petticoat government.* Jezebel ruled her husband, the monarch, and therefore she ruled the people of Israel.

Second, she was the one who initiated Baal worship. Jezebel's father, Ethbaal, was from Sidon; he was, in fact, king of the Sidonians. Baal worship, which originated with the Canaanites, had long existed in that area of the world. But the actual worship of Baal did not find its way into the hearts of the Israelites until it was introduced by marriage into Israel by Ahab. We might say, it was part of Jezebel's dowry. When Ahab married her, she brought her religious heritage with her: the idolatrous worship of Baal.

Baal was worshiped as the god of rain and fertility, who controlled the seasons, the crops, and the land. And when Baal worship entered the kingdom of Israel, bringing its heathen practices and barbaric sacrifices, the wickedness in the land only increased.

THE SUDDEN AND NEEDED PRESENCE OF A PROPHET

J. Oswald Sanders writes in an old work, *Robust in Faith*, "Elijah appeared at zero hour in Israel's history. . . . Like a meteor, he flashed across the inky blackness of Israel's spiritual night."² Nobody could have handled a couple like Ahab and Jezebel better than Elijah. The rugged, gaunt prophet from Tishbeh became God's instrument of confrontation.

F. B. Meyer calls Jezebel the Lady Macbeth of the Old Testament. She bore all of the markings of demon possession, and according to the record of her deeds, she was, in fact, Satan's woman of the hour.

In spiritual terms, this was a time of complete despair. The chasm between God and His people had reached its widest breadth. Imagine the thick demonic darkness as

> So he [Ahab] erected an altar for Baal in the house of Baal, which he built in Samaria.
>
> Ahab also made the Asherah. Ahab did more to provoke the Lord God of Israel than all the kings of Israel who were before him.
>
> 1 Kings 16:32–33

The Asherah represented the chief goddess of Tyre and, in the mythology of idolatry, the mother of Baal. The Asherim were pillars sculpted in the shape of Asherah, and all were associated with the worship of Baal.

As I read these words, I can almost hear the sigh in the narrative—the deep ache of the heart, written between the lines of the sacred text. And if you miss that, you miss the whole impact of Elijah's sudden, unannounced arrival.

> Now Elijah the Tishbite, who was of the settlers of Gilead, said to Ahab, "As the LORD, the God of Israel lives, before whom I stand, surely there shall be neither dew nor rain these years, except by my word."
>
> 1 Kings 17:1

Plunging full-force into the midst of this era of gross evil and wickedness is Elijah, God's heaven-sent prophet. A quick analysis of his introduction reveals three significant factors: his name, his origin, and his style.

His Name

The first thing that commands our attention is Elijah's name. The Hebrew word for "God" in the Old Testament is *Elohim,* which is occasionally abbreviated, *El.* The word *jah* is the word for "Jehovah." Thus, in Elijah's name we find the word for "God" and the word for "Jehovah." Between them is the small letter *I,* which in Hebrew has reference to the personal pronoun "my" or "mine." Putting the three together, then, we find that Elijah's name means "My God is Jehovah" or "The Lord is my God."

Ahab and Jezebel were in control of the land, and Baal was the god they worshiped. But when Elijah burst on the scene, his very name proclaimed: "I have one God. His name is Jehovah. He is the One I serve, before whom I stand."

As we said, the spiritual chasm between God and His people had reached its widest breadth. Elijah stood alone in that gap.

His Land

The second point of significance is Elijah's place of origin. Elijah was from Tishbeh; therefore, he's called "Elijah the Tishbite." Remember that we know very little about Tishbeh, not even its exact location. However, the text does indicate that it was in Gilead, which was in the northern Transjordan area—that is, on the eastern side of the Jordan River. Given this clue, historians have pieced a few details together with the help of the archaeologists' spade.

Gilead was a place of solitude and outdoor life, a place where people would likely have been rugged, tanned from the sun, muscular and leathery. It was never a place of polish, sophistication, and diplomacy. It was an austere land, and one senses that Elijah's appearance was in keeping with that. His manner might have bordered on coarse and crude, rough and rugged—not unlike many of the great fiery characters God has introduced at certain times to an unsuspecting world. These characters may not win many friends, but one thing is certain: They cannot be ignored. Prophets are always like that.

In his masterful work *Great Voices of the Reformation*, Harry Emerson Fosdick gives us just such a portrait of the great fiery prophet of Scotland, John Knox:

> Knox was a stern man in a stern age in a rough and violent country. Says Dr. Thomas McCrie: "The corruptions by which Christianity was universally disfigured before the Reformation had grown to a greater height in Scotland than in any other nation within the pale of the Western church. Superstition and religious imposture in their grossest forms, gained an easy admission among a rude and ignorant people." From the first, Knox's road was rough, and it took a rough man to travel it. . . . Others snipped at the branches of the Papistry; but he strikes at the root, to destroy the whole.[3]

But Knox also had a gentle and tender side. It was said that sometimes when he opened the Word of God, "he could not speak a word for his tears." It was also said that the queen "feared the pen of John Knox more than the armies of Scotland." He was a man of letters—a man of moving tenderness—*and* a prophet unafraid and unintimidated. It took that kind of man to meet that grim hour in Scotland.

And it took a man like Elijah to meet this hour in Israel's history. An austere, solitary man from the rugged village of Tishbeh.

His Style

Elijah's name was significant, as were his roots. But what comes most immediately to mind when I think of Elijah is his style. Right from the get-go, he's in the king's face. Without a moment's hesitation, with no apparent fear or reluctance, Elijah stands before Ahab the king and comes right to the point.

Now remember, the kingdom of Israel has known sixty or more years of unbelief, assassinations, idolatry, ungodliness, and cutthroat rulers. Furthermore, the present king and his dominating partner are the worst of the lot. Onto this stage steps a prophet from nowhere. He follows no protocol, makes no introductions, offers no deference to the royal presence. He is without sophistication, polish, training, or courtly manners. He simply announces, "As the LORD, the God of Israel lives, before whom I stand, surely there shall be neither dew nor rain these years, except by my word."

Elijah is a man on a mission, declaring himself a servant of "the Lord, the God of Israel," when all around him are evidences of blatant Baal worship. Without preparing his audience for the warning, he makes the ominous pronouncement: "No rain—not even dew—for years, unless I say so." His words sound so matter of fact, but keep in mind, he's shaking his fist in the devil's face. He's setting the record straight. As we say in Texas, "It's time to fish or cut bait." Baal or no Baal, folks, Elijah says, you're not getting any rain. And without rain, you don't have crops. Your cattle will die. People will die. It's curtains.

Elijah delivers the goods. He's a stand-in-the-gap messenger, uniquely anointed and used by God. He travels solo, sounding the alarm, trying to awaken an indifferent and even hostile populace.

WHEN YOU STAND ALONE

Today there are still those who stand alone in the gap, those who still strive to shake us awake. A handful of brave students at Columbine High School come immediately to mind. Loaded guns and the threat of death couldn't silence them. I think of them as modern-day Elijahs, whom God uses to deliver a life-changing message. Men and women of courage, ready to stand and deliver. Authentic heroes.

Elijah, David, Esther, Moses, and Joseph, along with Knox, Lee, and others—not a mediocre bone in their bodies. These were men and women who were willing to stand alone against the strongest forces of their day and, without reluctance or embarrassment, proclaim the name of the Lord.

Do you remember what God led another of His great prophets to write about this?

> And I searched for a man among them who should build up the wall and stand in the gap before Me for the land, that I should not destroy it; but I found no one.
>
> Ezekiel 22:30

The quest continues. Our Lord is still searching for people who will make a difference. Christians dare not be mediocre. We dare not dissolve into the background or blend into the neutral scenery of this world. Sometimes you have to look awfully close and talk awfully long before an individual will declare his allegiance to God. Sometimes you have to look long and hard to find someone with the courage to stand alone for God. Is that what we have created today in this age of tolerance and compromise?

Elijah's life teaches us what the Lord requires.

LESSONS LEARNED FROM A GAP-STANDING PROPHET

Several lasting lessons emerge from Elijah's example.

First: God looks for special people at difficult times. God needed a special man to shine the light in the blackness of those days. But God didn't find him in the palace or the court. He didn't find him walking around with his head down in the school of the prophets. He didn't even find him in the homes of the ordinary people. God found him in Tishbeh, of all places. A man who would stand in the gap couldn't be suave or slick; he had to be tough.

God looked for somebody who had the backbone to stand alone. Someone who had the courage to say, "That's wrong!" Someone who could stand toe to toe with an idolater and proclaim, "God is God."

In our culture—our schools, our offices and factories, our lunchrooms and boardrooms, our halls of ivy and our halls of justice—we need men and women of God, young people of God. We need respected professionals, athletes, homemakers, teachers, public figures, and private citizens who will promote the things of God, who will stand alone—stand tall, stand firm, stand strong!

How's your stature and your integrity? Have you corrupted your principles just to stay in business? To get a good grade? To make the team? To be with the *in* crowd? To earn the next rank or promotion? Have you winked at language or behavior that a few years ago would have horrified you? Are you, right now, compromising morally because you don't want to be considered a prude?

Those who find comfort in the court of Ahab can never bring themselves to stand in the gap with Elijah.

Second: God's methods are often surprising. God did not raise up an army to destroy Ahab and Jezebel. Neither did He send some scintillating prince to argue His case or try to impress their royal majesties. Instead God did the unimaginable—He chose somebody like . . . well, like Elijah.

Are you thinking right now that somebody else is better qualified for that short-term mission assignment? For that leadership training group? For that community service?

Are you a wife and homemaker who feels that your contribution to God's service is not noteworthy? Do you see other people as *special* or *called* or *talented?*

You may be missing a ministry opportunity that is right there in front of you. You may be in the very midst of a ministry and not even realize it. (What greater ministry can there be, for example, than that of a faithful and loving wife and mother?) Your ministry may be to just two or three people and that's all. Don't discount that. God's methods are often surprising. In fact, at times I have found them even illogical. They don't really make good sense to our finite minds. David's brothers laughed at the thought of his standing against Goliath. And what about Joshua walking around the walls of Jericho and blowing those trumpets? We're talking strange, folks.

Third: We stand before God. When we're standing alone in the gap, ultimately, we're standing before God. When the call comes, will God find us ready and willing to stand for Him? Will He find in us hearts that are completely His? Will He be able to say, "Ah, yes, that one's heart is completely Mine. Yes, there's sufficient commitment there for Me to use that life with an Ahab. That's the kind of devotion I'm looking for."

If your Christianity hasn't put that kind of steel in your spine, that quality of marrow in your bones, there's something terribly wrong, either with the message you're hearing or with your heart. God is looking for men and women whose hearts are completely His, men and women who won't blend into the scenery.

When I was in high school, one of my favorite courses was drama. On our drama team we had a young red-haired fellow named Sam, who was so good in every part he took that he easily outshone the rest of us. He was so good, in fact, that he soon became the object of much jealousy among many of the other budding thespians. This became such a problem that, when it came time for the senior play in Sam's senior year, the director, who was getting so much flak, finally said, "Okay, I'm just gonna give him the part of the butler."

Now the butler did not have one spoken line in the play. The only thing he had to do was stand in the same place in every act, every scene, throughout the play. Not much you can do with a part like that, right?

Well, guess what: Sam still got the award for best actor in the senior play. He didn't have one line, but what a range of expressions he gave the audience—such caricatures, such faces, such movements. In fact, the play was a flop except for him. Even as a butler, without one line, he did not blend into the scenery of nothingness.

No matter what role you fill in life, you're not unimportant when it comes to standing alone for truth.

What spot has God given you? Whatever it is, God says, "You're standing before *Me,* and I want to use you. I want to use you as My unique spokesperson in your day and age, at this moment and time."

Elijah, this gaunt, rugged figure striding out of nowhere, suddenly stepping into the pages of history, is a clear witness of the value of one life completely committed to God. An unknown man from a backwater place, he was called to stand against evil in the most turbulent and violent and decadent of times.

Look around. The need is still great, and God is still searching.

Now Elijah the Tishbite, who was of the settlers of Gilead, said to Ahab, "As the LORD, *the God of Israel lives, before whom I stand, surely there shall be neither dew nor rain these years, except by my word." And the word of the* LORD *came to him, saying, "Go away from here and turn eastward, and hide yourself by the brook Cherith, which is east of the Jordan. And it shall be that you shall drink of the brook, and I have commanded the ravens to provide for you there." So he went and did according to the word of the* LORD, *for he went and lived by the brook Cherith, which is east of the Jordan. And the ravens brought him bread and meat in the morning and bread and meat in the evening, and he would drink from the brook. And it happened after a while, that the brook dried up, because there was no rain in the land.*

1 KINGS 17:1–7

CHAPTER TWO

Boot Camp at Cherith

"I am going to cut you down to size!" If I heard that once during the ten weeks I spent in a U.S. Marine Corps boot camp over forty years ago, I must have heard it a dozen times. As I recall, those words formed the theme of the opening speech, delivered with passion, by a man I quickly learned to obey. Those words still play back to me in my mind, and the shrill tone of my drill instructor's voice remains a vivid memory. He meant every word he said, and he kept his promise.

There we stood, an unorganized, ragtag bunch of seventy or so young men of every conceivable size and background, thrown together in a strange place, having no idea (thankfully) what was ahead of us. During the months that followed, every shred of self-sufficient arrogance, every hint of independent spirit, and all thought of rebellion was scraped away. Any indifference toward authority was replaced by a firm commitment to do only as we were told, regardless. We learned to survive in the crucible of intense, extreme training that has characterized the Marine Corps throughout its proud and proven history.

The disciplined regimen of boot camp—day after day, week after week—

brought about remarkable changes in each one of us. As a result, we left that place completely different than we were when we arrived. The isolation of our location, the absence of all soft creature comforts, the relentless, monotonous drills and demanding repetition of inspections, the tests that forced us to encounter the unknown without showing fear (all mixed with the maddening determination and constant harassment of our drill instructor), yielded powerful dividends. Almost without realizing it, while learning to submit ourselves to the commands of our leader, we ultimately found ourselves physically fit, emotionally stirred, and mentally ready for whatever conflict might come our way . . . even the harsh reality of facing the enemy in combat.

That kind of raw recruit training is precisely what the Lord had in mind when He sent His servant Elijah from the court of King Ahab to the brook Cherith. Little did the prophet know that his being hidden away at Cherith would prove to be *his* boot camp experience. There, he would be trained to trust his Leader so that he might ultimately do battle with a treacherous enemy. To accomplish this, the Lord would "cut him down to size" at Cherith.

> And the word of the Lord came to him, saying, "Go away from here and turn eastward, and hide yourself by the brook Cherith, which is east of the Jordan.
>
> "And it shall be that you shall drink of the brook, and I have commanded the ravens to provide for you there."
>
> So he went and did according to the word of the Lord, for he went and lived by the brook Cherith, which is east of the Jordan.
>
> 1 Kings 17:2–5

As we read those words and try to imagine the original setting, we begin to see the surprising nature of God's plan. The most logical arrangement, seemingly, would be to keep Elijah in the king's face—to use the prophet as a persistent goad, pressing the godless monarch into submission, forcing him to surrender his will to the One who had created him. After all, none of King Ahab's advisors and counselors had Elijah's integrity. There was no one nearby to confront the king's idolatrous ways or his cruel and unfair acts against the people of Israel. It only made good sense to leave Elijah there in the court of the king.

So much for human logic.

God's plan is always full of surprise and mystery. I have written of this at length elsewhere, so here I will only underscore the fact of the recurring, seemingly inexplicable plan of God. While *we* might have chosen to leave Elijah there, standing toe to toe with Ahab, such was not the Father's plan. He had things He wished to accomplish deep within His servant's inner life, things that would prepare Elijah for encounters that might destroy a less-obedient, less-committed, and less-prepared servant. Hence, God immediately sent him away to a place of isolation, hidden from everyone, where he would not only be protected from physical danger but would also be better prepared for a greater mission.

For the godly hero to be useful as an instrument of significance in the Lord's hand, he must be humbled and forced to trust. He must, in other words, be "cut down to size." Or, as A. W. Tozer loved to say, "It's doubtful that God can bless a man greatly until He has hurt him deeply."[1] It has been my observation over the years that the deeper the hurt, the greater the usefulness.

Often in the Old Testament the original names of places carry symbolic meanings. This is certainly the case with this Hebrew term "Cherith." Although today no one can identify the location of that brook, we do know that it derived its name from the original verb *Cha-rath,* which means "to cut off, to cut down." The word is used both ways in the Old Testament: as in being cut off from others or from the blessings of a covenant; and also of being cut down, as one might cut down tall timber. Thus, while at Cherith, the man who had been a spokesman for God as he stood before Ahab would be "cut off" from all involvement and activities that might prove stimulating to him. At the same time, Elijah would be "cut down" to size as his Lord used that uncomfortable situation to force him to trust Him for each day's needs.

You see, there was one problem at this point: Elijah was a spokesman, but he was not yet, truly, a man of God. Let's examine why I say that. In

1 Kings 17:1 the writer describes Elijah as simply "Elijah the Tishbite." He came out of nowhere and suddenly stood before the king to deliver God's message. But by verse 24, as a result of his basic training experiences at Camp Cherith, he is addressed as "a man of God."

At the beginning of the chapter he is simply Elijah from the town of Tishbeh, somewhere in Gilead. But by the end of the chapter he emerges as *a man of God*. In between verses 1 and 24 is what I like to call Elijah's boot camp experience. So let's look at what that experience meant in the prophet's life.

THE PROLONGED DROUGHT

When he first comes on the scene, Elijah, as God's mouthpiece, stands before King Ahab and announces that a drought is coming. But this will be no ordinary drought.

> Now Elijah the Tishbite ... said to Ahab, "As the LORD, the God of Israel lives, before whom I stand, surely there shall be neither dew nor rain these years, except by my word."
>
> 1 Kings 17:1

This simple, unknown spokesman, the man from nowhere, stands before the most powerful man in the land, whose domineering wife, Jezebel—the power behind the throne—is determined to rid Israel of all the prophets of Jehovah. Jezebel "destroyed the prophets of the LORD," says 1 Kings 18:4, killing them off as carelessly as she would swat flies. Nevertheless, Elijah, standing in front of Ahab, states unequivocally, "There will be a famine for years." And by announcing his source of information as "the LORD, the God of Israel," he is clearly defying Ahab's self-appointed importance.

Between the lines, of course, Elijah is saying, "Let's get this straight right here and now, Ahab! You are not the most powerful person in the land. That position is reserved for the living God of heaven, Jehovah, who is the sovereign Ruler over all. Can you stop the rain? No way. But He can. He can lock up those rain clouds for as long as He chooses." In fact, the prophet holds nothing back as he announces, "There will be neither dew nor rain these years, except by my word."

As I try to put myself in Ahab's sandals, the word that grabs my attention in Elijah's statement is "years." The people of Israel could withstand a drought for a few weeks, perhaps even a few months. The wells would not dry up immediately, and the natural cisterns in the rocks, storing up rainwater and runoff, would tide them over during normal dry spells. Lack of rainfall in that arid region would not have been unusual. But we're not talking about weeks or months. We're talking about years. "There will be no dew or rain for these *years*," said Elijah. "Not until the Lord God directs me to give the word will relief come."

There's no getting around it. This is a life-threatening pronouncement.

Now at this point I have to think that Elijah wanted to hit the streets running, declaring doom from house to house, warning the people: "God is trying to get your attention! Listen to the word of God! There is going to be a lengthy, devastating drought!" But God didn't tell him to do that. Instead, God sent His prophet to spend some time in isolation at boot camp.

In doing so, God moved Elijah from the palace to His personally chosen hideaway, from the public forum to the private haven, from the sunlight of activity to the shadows of obscurity.

INTO THE SHADOWS

Any recruit who has been through boot camp can tell you that every hour of the day someone is ordering you where to go, when to be there, what to do, and how to survive. That's a vital part of basic training. And God did the same for His prophet. He told Elijah exactly where he was to go, what he was to do when he got there, and how he would manage to survive. How strange the plan must have seemed to Elijah.

The first thing he was to do was *hide*.

"Go away from here and turn eastward, and hide yourself by the brook Cherith, which is east of the Jordan.

1 Kings 17:3

"Hide myself? I'm a prophet! I'm a palace man. I'm out there in public proclaiming your Word. You seem to forget, Lord, I'm called to preach." No, God told Elijah. Not this time. "Hide yourself," God said.

The Hebrew word here suggests the idea of concealment, of being absent on purpose. "Conceal yourself, Elijah," God said. "Absent yourself in secrecy."

One of the most difficult commands to hear, and one of the hardest commands to obey is the command to hide. The admonition to go off and be alone, to get away from the public spotlight, to drop back and deliberately remain hidden. This is especially true if you are comfortable in the limelight, an up-front kind of person, one who is obviously gifted with leadership abilities. It's also true if you are a *doer*. A get-the-job-done kind of person.

You may be a capable woman, whether homemaker or career woman. Then, suddenly, you are snatched from your world of endless activity and effective involvement. God says, in no uncertain terms, "Hide yourself. Get alone. Get out of the limelight. Get away from all those things that satisfy your human pride and ego and go live by the brook."

Sometimes sickness forces such a change. Sometimes we reach the peak of our energy output and begin to burn out, or we are about to do so. Sometimes God simply removes us from one place and reshapes us for another.

God had two reasons for commanding Elijah to hide himself. First, He wanted to protect Elijah from Ahab; and second, He wanted to train him to become a man of God. When God says to us, almost out of the blue, "Hide yourself," He usually has both purposes in mind: protection and training.

GOD'S PROVISIONS

The first thing God does after He sends Elijah to Camp Cherith is tell him how he's going to survive. This is going to be a tough and lonely experience, a survivalist adventure; therefore, God gives Elijah this remarkable promise:

"And it shall be that you shall drink of the brook, and I have commanded the ravens to provide for you there."

1 Kings 17:4

The ravens will be God's catering service, bringing provisions to His prophet. "The ravens will bring in your food, Elijah." Isn't that incredible?

Imagine what a conversation with Elijah might have been like at that point. As he leaves Ahab's palace and heads down the street, knapsack slung over his back, someone calls out, "Where are you going, Elijah?"

"I'm outta here . . . on my way to the hills."

"Where are you gonna stay?"

"Some place called Cherith. There's a small brook running through it."

"Cherith? Where's that?"

"I'm not really sure. God's gonna show me. I think it's over there, east of the Jordan somewhere."

"What are you gonna do there?"

"Well, for one thing, I'm gonna drink from that brook."

"The brook! What will you have to eat?"

"Actually, God told me the birds are going to bring my food."

God makes provision for Elijah's physical welfare during this time of seclusion. But He also provides for his spiritual welfare. God knew what Elijah needed; therefore, the silence and solitude were to be essential parts of his boot camp experience.

A. W. Pink, writing on Elijah, says this:

> The prophet needed further training in secret if he was to be personally fitted to speak again for God in public. . . . The man whom the Lord uses has to be kept low: severe discipline has to be experienced by him. . . . Three more years must be spent by the prophet in seclusion. How humbling! Alas, how little is man to be trusted: how little is he able to bear being put into the place of honor! How quickly self rises to the surface, and the instrument is ready to believe he is something more than an instrument. How sadly easy it is to make of the very service God entrusts us with a pedestal on which to display ourselves.[2]

In essence, God said to Elijah, "You need to get out of the spotlight. You need to come up in the mountains, alone with Me, where you can hear my voice clearly. We need more time together, Elijah, and you need more training."

The good news is this: Without one moment's hesitation, Elijah obeyed. He didn't even ask why.

> So he went and did according to the word of the LORD, for he went and lived by the brook Cherith, which is east of the Jordan.
>
> 1 Kings 17:5

Notice the wording here. He went and *lived* by the brook Cherith. It's one thing to take a day trip off the beaten track, or to go camping for a weekend, or even to spend two or three weeks backpacking in the wilderness. Such adventures offer all the delights of being away from the cares of the *real world* for a time, even as you have the comfort of knowing that your lifeline to civilization is still there. It's quite another thing to *live* in the wilderness, alone, for an extended time. But that's exactly what Elijah did for months, possibly the better part of a year. God said, "Go there. Settle there. Live there." And that's what Elijah did.

Would you accept such an assignment from God with such immediate obedience? How many of us would say nothing except, "Yes, Sir. I trust You completely. I don't need the spotlight to survive." Or do we enjoy only comfortable and active Christianity?

While there is certainly nothing wrong with being a leader or fulfilling the role of spokesman for God, how easy it is to become addicted to the public forum, or to feel that we are indispensable to God's plan. How easy to neglect, ignore or overlook those occasions when we need to pull back, regroup, rethink, and renew our souls.

ELIJAH'S RESPONSE

Whether in the palace or in private, Elijah was ready to serve His Lord. Whether in the spotlight or in silence, he was satisfied to be lost in the secrecy of the quiet hills beside a brook east of the Jordan. And there, God supplied his needs.

> And the ravens brought him bread and meat in the morning and bread and meat in the evening, and he would drink from the brook.
>
> 1 Kings 17:6

What an incredible experience that must have been! A bit of bread and meat in the morning, another small sandwich in the evening, and throughout the day the cool, refreshing water from the brook. If you've ever traveled in Israel and the area across the Jordan, you know how precious water is in that land at any time, let alone during a time of drought. Yet God provided His prophet with a fresh, trickling brook of water. Any time he wanted to, he could get down on his belly and cup his hands around that cool, sweet water of life in that dry and thirsty land.

But we can't always live by the bubbling brook. This is not Fantasyland, remember; this is hard-core boot camp. Times of extensive training and intense testing are required courses in God's character-building curriculum.

> And it happened after a while, that the brook dried up, because there was no rain in the land.
>
> 1 Kings 17:7

One morning Elijah noticed that the brook wasn't gushing over the rocks or bubbling as freely as it had in days past. Since that single stream of water was his lifeline, he checked it carefully. Over the next few days he watched it dwindle and shrink, until it was only a trickle. Then one morning, there was no water, only wet sand. The hot winds soon siphoned even that dampness, and the sand hardened. Before long, cracks appeared in the parched bed of the brook. No more water. The brook had dried up.

Does that boot camp experience sound familiar to any of you? At one time you knew the joy of a full bank account, a booming business, an exciting, ever-expanding career, a magnificent ministry. But . . . the brook has dried up.

At one time you knew the joy of using your voice to sing the Lord's praises. Then a growth developed on your vocal chords, requiring surgery. But the surgery removed more than the growth; it also took your lovely singing voice. The brook has dried up.

You finished college, stepped into a promising profession, and surrounded yourself with stimulating, gifted individuals. At the zenith of your career, things changed. Money got tight. Your best friends moved away. Most are now gone and the future is bleak. The brook has dried up.

Your company has moved you to another location, and you've had to leave the church that has been home for many years. The great music you once enjoyed is but a memory. The pulpit ministry is weak. Your kids are dissatisfied. The brook has dried up.

Your partner in life has grown indifferent and has recently asked for a divorce. There's no longer any affection and no promise of change. The brook has dried up.

I've had my own times when the brook has dried up, and I've found myself wondering about the things I've believed and preached for years. What happened? Had God died? No. My vision just got a little blurry. My circumstances caused my thinking to get a little foggy. I looked up, and I couldn't see Him as clearly. To exacerbate the problem, I felt as though He wasn't hearing me. The heavens were like brass. I would speak to Him and nothing came back. My brook dried up.

That's what happened to John Bunyan back in the seventeenth century in England. He preached against the godlessness of his day, and the authorities shoved him into prison. His brook of opportunity and freedom dried up. But because Bunyan firmly believed God was still alive and working, he turned that prison into a place of praise, service and creativity as he began to write *Pilgrim's Progress,* the most famous allegory in the history of the English language. Dried-up brooks in no way cancel out God's providential plan. Often, they cause it to emerge.

LESSONS FOR ELIJAH AND FOR US

Elijah was in a tough spot. A life-threatening spot. The brook had dried up. Had God forgotten His faithful servant? Has God forgotten you? Has He left you all alone?

Before going any further, this is a good place to pause and reflect. Two lessons come to mind as I consider this segment of Elijah's life. *First, the God who gives water can also withhold water.* That's His sovereign right.

Our human feelings tell us that once our faithful heavenly Father gives water, He should never take it away. It just wouldn't be fair. Once God gives a mate, He should never take a mate. Once God gives a child, He should never take a child. Once He gives a good business, He has no right to take that business. Once He provides a pastor, He must never call him elsewhere. Once He gives us growth and delight in a ministry, He has no right to step in and say, "Wait a minute. There's no need to grow larger. Let Me take you deeper instead."

When we hit a tough spot, our tendency is to feel abandoned, to become resentful, to think, *How could God forget me?* In fact, just the opposite is true, for at that moment, we are more than ever the object of His concern.

Now I don't know how Elijah felt or what he thought when he first saw that dry streambed, but I do know from experience that when our brook dries up, two things are certain: (1) God is still alive and well! and (2) He knows what He's doing!

Three verses from Isaiah's pen ministered to me at a time when my brook had slowed to a trickle, then finally dried up. These verses became an encouraging reminder of who is in control, and they stopped me short of becoming resentful.

> But Zion said, "The LORD has forsaken me,
> And the Lord has forgotten me."
>
> "Can a woman forget her nursing child,
> And have no compassion on the son of her womb?
> Even these may forget, but I will not forget you.

Behold, I have inscribed you on the palms of My hands;
Your walls are continually before Me."

Isaiah 49:14–16

"The Lord has forsaken me . . . He has walked away . . . He has totally forgotten me." Ever said that? Of course you have! How about on Monday morning? You've just come off a glorious weekend retreat. Time in the Word. Great worship. Sustained, in-depth fellowship with other believers. Lots of laughter. Meaningful prayer. Your brook is flowing rapidly. Then comes eight o'clock Monday morning back home, and your whole *world* caves in. "The Lord's forgotten me. He's completely left the scene."

But God says, in the midst of your dried-up brook, "You are written on the palms of My hands. You are continually before me." Then He uses that wonderful image of a young mother with her new baby . . . and He surprises us with a realistic reminder: "Can a woman forget her nursing child?" You wouldn't think so, would you? But look at the stories in the news, and you know how many women do exactly that. Babies left in garbage dumpsters. Tiny babies abandoned—sometimes even abused or tortured or murdered. Yes, as unimaginable as it seems, even a mother *can* forget her nursing child. But here's the clincher: Not God. Not God! He will *never* forget us. We are permanently inscribed on the palms of His hands.

Stop and glance at the palms of your hand. Now, imagine they are God's hands and that you are right there. The Amplified Bible renders Isaiah 49:16 this way: "I have indelibly imprinted (tattooed) a picture of you on the palm of each of my hands." Our ways remain continually before Him. Not one fleeting moment of life goes by without His knowing exactly where we are, what we're doing, and how we're feeling. God never has to frown and look around, saying, "Now where in the world did Chuck go? I've misplaced that man again." Oh, no. I'm right there in the palm of His hand. And so are you.

And when we end up beside a dry streambed, He never has to admit, "Oops, now how did he wind up there?" No. God says, "That's right. That's exactly where I want you. Yes. Perfect."

"But it hurts, Lord. I remember when times were so much easier . . . when I drank from this brook. I feel so displaced."

"I know it, but it's where I want you. I see you there. I haven't forgotten you. Trust me through this."

I can still remember when I went through the transition, back in 1994, of leaving a magnificent, almost twenty-three-year ministry in Fullerton, California, and beginning a whole new career at Dallas Seminary. What a change. I left pastoring a vibrant, growing, cutting-edge local church, surrounded by a staff of over twenty men and women God had called to work alongside one another, to work in an academic setting with folks I hardly knew. (Great people—just like the ones I'd left—but we didn't know one another.) We left a home our family had lived in for years, long-established roots, easy-going relationships, and familiar daily routines. My once-bubbling brook was drying up. Everything familiar was only a memory.

And talk about *lonely!* My wife, Cynthia, stayed in California to continue her leadership at our Insight for Living ministry, to sell our wonderful home, and then to pack up our belongings and handle all the other details connected with such a major move. Meanwhile, I was working in Dallas and staying in a tiny garage apartment, thanks to the generosity of some wonderful friends. Cynthia and I saw each other on weekends, usually, but sometimes our responsibilities wouldn't allow even that. How displaced I felt . . . and occasionally, strangely abandoned by God. Every now and then my mind played tricks on me. *I'm all alone!* I thought.

My brook dried up.

Had God forsaken us? Of course not! Were we abandoned? Not for a split second. Was He aware of our circumstance . . . did He care? *Yes!* He knew exactly where we were. He also knew that I, approaching sixty years of age at that time, needed another session of basic training at Camp Cherith. He needed to remind me that it was time to learn again to trust Him—and Him alone, in the midst of the adjustments, the loneliness, and the unfamiliarity of my surroundings. *Everything!*

Looking back, I am *so* thankful for that time of transition. How *many* things He taught Cynthia and me about Himself. How amazed we are—

how thrilled we are—to see how He's used us here. How grateful! God had not forgotten us.

God hadn't forgotten Elijah either—over there on the east side of the Jordan beside the brook called Cherith, which had become a dried-up streambed of sand and rock. And here's where the *second lesson* comes at this moment in Elijah's life, because *that dried-up brook was a direct result of Elijah's own prayer.*

> Elijah was a man with a nature like ours, and he prayed earnestly that it might not rain; and it did not rain on the earth for three years and six months.
>
> James 5:17

According to that statement in the New Testament letter of James, Elijah had prayed that it would not rain, and ultimately, it would not rain for three and a half years. So the dried-up brook was just an indication that the very thing he had prayed for was beginning to take place. He was living in the result of his own prayer.

Have you ever had that happen? "Lord, make me a godly man. Lord, mold me into a woman after your own heart." Meanwhile, in your heart you're thinking, *but don't let it hurt too much.* "Lord, make me stable, long-suffering, and gracious," *but don't remove too many of my creature comforts.* "Lord, teach me faith, make me strong," *but don't let me suffer.* Have you ever bargained with God like that? We want instant maturity, not the kind that requires sacrifice or emotional pain or hardship. "Lord, give me patience . . . *and I want it right now!*"

God's spiritual boot camp doesn't work that way. It is designed for our development toward maturity, not for our comfort. But self-denial is not a popular virtue in today's culture.

A short time before Robert E. Lee passed into his Lord's presence, a young mother brought her tiny infant to him. With tenderness, Lee took the child and held him in his arms, looking deeply into the baby's eyes. He then looked up at the mother and said, "Teach him he must deny himself."

The seasoned veteran knew whereof he spoke. As Douglas Southall

Freeman writes, "Had his [Lee's] life been epitomized in one sentence of the Book he read so often, it would have been in the words, 'If any man will come after Me, let him deny himself, and take up his cross daily, and follow Me.'"[3]

Our God is relentless. He never ceases His training regimens. He shaves off our hair, He takes away our comfortable and secure lifestyle, He moves us into cramped and unfamiliar quarters, and He changes our circle of friends—just like Marine boot camp!

In the process, He strips us of *all* our pride! And then He begins to lay the foundation blocks of heroic courage, and a new kind of pride, if you will—the kind that no longer defends us but defends Him. What a magnificent change that is. And how essential in our journey toward maturity! It's all part of being *cut down to size.*

FOUR LESSONS FROM CHERITH

Let's not leave the obscure setting of Cherith with its now dried-up brook and the young prophet's being made into a man of God without seeing the truths revealed there.

First: We must be as willing to be set aside as we are to be used. F. B. Meyer calls this "the value of the hidden life."[4]

This truth is captured vividly in the words of the old hymn:

> "Speak, Lord, in the stillness,
> While I wait on Thee;
> Hushed my heart to listen
> In expectancy."[5]

We must be willing to be set aside so that we can listen for God's voice in the stillness . . . away from the cacophony of everyday life, away from our own busyness, our own agendas, our own desires. We need to learn the deep and enduring value of the hidden life.

When I think of hidden lives, I think of mothers of small children. I think of compassionate men and women who are now caring for elderly parents. I think of highly capable or qualified individuals, who, it seems, for the time being, are completely useless. I think of students still in the classroom, preparing, preparing, preparing. It's the hidden life—the life where lasting lessons are learned.

Second: God's direction includes God's provision. God says, "Go to the brook. I will provide."

Vance Havner, in his book, *It Is Toward Evening,* tells the story of a group of farmers who were raising cotton in the Deep South when the devastating boll weevil invaded the crops. These men had put all of their savings, dedicated all of their fields, set all of their hopes in cotton. Then the boll weevil came. Before long, it looked as if they were headed for the poorhouse.

But farmers, being the determined and ingenious people they are, decided, "Well, we can't plant cotton, so let's plant peanuts." Amazingly, those peanuts brought them more money than they would have ever made raising cotton.

When the farmers realized that what had seemed like a disaster had actually proved to be a boon, they erected a large and impressive monument to the boll weevil—a monument to the very thing they thought would destroy them.

"Sometimes we settle into a humdrum routine as monotonous as growing cotton year after year," says Havner, himself a seasoned old saint of God at the time he wrote these words. "Then God sends the boll weevil; He jolts us out of our groove, and we must find new ways to live. Financial reverses, great bereavement, physical infirmity, loss of position—how many have been driven by trouble to be better husbandmen and to bring forth far finer fruit from their souls! The best thing that ever happened to some of us was the coming of our 'boll weevil.'"[6]

When God directs, God provides. That's what sustained Elijah during his boot camp experience.

Third: We have to learn to trust God one day at a time. I know some of you are saying to yourself, "Oh, Chuck, I've heard that a hundred times." But until you're living it, you haven't heard it enough. You must learn to live today . . . today. You cannot live tomorrow today, or next week tomorrow.

"The reason so many of us are overwrought, tense, distracted, and anxious is that we've never mastered the art of living one day at a time," writes William Elliott in *For the Living of These Days*. "Physically we do live a day at a time. We can't quite help ourselves. But mentally we live in all three tenses at once . . . and that will not work!"[7]

Did you notice that God never told Elijah what the second step would be until he had taken the first step? God told His prophet to go to Ahab. When Elijah got to the palace, God told him what to say. After he said it, God told him, "Now, go to the brook." He didn't tell Elijah what was going to happen at Cherith; he just said, "Go to the brook and hide yourself." Elijah didn't know the future, but he did have God's promise: "I'll provide for you there." And God didn't tell him the next step until the brook had dried up.

That leads to our fourth lesson.

Fourth: A dried-up brook is often a sign of God's pleasure, not disappointment, in your life. Now if you miss that, you miss it all. The dried-up brook is usually a sign of God's acceptance of us, not His judgment.

Right at the height of his career, when he was becoming known as a great man of God, Abraham was told by the Lord, "Take Isaac and put him on the altar and kill him." I would say that qualifies as Abraham's brook drying up, wouldn't you? Yet God was intensely pleased with His servant Abraham.

Right in the middle of Paul's remarkably successful first missionary journey, he was stoned at Lystra and left for dead. His brook dried up . . . but that dark day became one of the turning points in his life.

Joseph was thrown into an Egyptian dungeon after being falsely accused and misjudged. During that extremely painful time, Joseph's brook dried up. Did it mean God was displeased? On the contrary, God was well pleased with his servant Joseph. But He had some things of great value for Joseph to learn in that prison of silence and solitude, removed from the limelight and separated from everyday life in a world of freedom.

Remember, even Jesus our Lord, the sinless Son of God, had to pass through the anguish of Gethsemane.

OUR OBSTACLE COURSE

Part of every boot camp experience is the grueling, grinding, and sometimes daunting obstacle course. It is neither fun nor easy, but its demanding discipline prepares the recruit for whatever situations he or she may face in the future, particularly under enemy fire. In the spiritual life, before we can truly benefit from "the hidden life" that God uses to prepare us for whatever future He has planned for us, we must overcome at least four major obstacles. I think of them as four tough membranes of the flesh: pride, fear, resentment, and long-standing habits. Conquering these layers of resistance will prepare us for the future and harden us for combat with the enemy of our soul.

Pride. God begins to work on our pride as He removes us from the limelight. This is part of the necessary process involved in cutting us down to size. Initially, we fight against it, and in our resistance, we may become disillusioned and confused. We struggle because we've gotten used to the bright lights of public attention and the ego-satisfying applause, but God persists, as He did with Elijah, in hiding us away. As John the Baptizer would learn many centuries later, "He must increase, but I must decrease" (John 3:30). *We learn submission* through this painful process.

Fear. When hidden away for an undisclosed period of time, we encounter another carnal layer of inner resistance: fear. God uses the loss of position, the loss of prestige, the loss of popularity, the loss of privileges to reveal this layer. Then, as He breaks through that barrier, He introduces us to new depths of maturity. At this stage of the obstacle course, as our fears are overcome, *we learn to walk by faith.*

Resentment. Inevitably, however, this painful process will uncover a layer of resentment. This is prompted by anger as we're forced to release those rights to which we think we are entitled: the rights to the kind of salary we think we ought to be getting; the rights to the kind of treatment we deserve; the rights to the comforts we should enjoy. Our resentment intensifies! It says, "I have my rights!" But God just continues to grind and work down to the quick, until finally we say, "Okay, okay, I release it all to You!" At that point, *we learn forgiveness.* Resentment, I've found, usually stems from a lack of forgiveness.

Habit. Finally, God uses His obstacle course of faith to break through our layer of long-standing habits—those deep-seated attitudes we have formed during busy years of active service, high (often unrealistic) expectations, and success-oriented motives that only feed our carnality. All that is ultimately stripped away, and at this stage we begin to understand what God has wrought: The total renovation of our inner being. And it is here that *we learn humility*—the crowning accomplishment of God's inner working.

This process is the secret to becoming a godly man or woman. Pride, fear, resentment, and habit are all tough evidences of the flesh. But those who are being shaped into the image of Christ do not go the way of the flesh. Women and men of God do not manipulate events so that they can be pleased and get what they want. That's why God crushes pride, removes fear, breaks into resentment, and changes long-standing habits until the whole inner being is renovated . . . until we rest in our God and are ready for His will, not ours, to be done.

Ella Wheeler Wilcox captures the essence of this in her poem, *Gethsemane:*

> Down shadowy lanes, across strange streams
> Bridged over by our broken dreams;
> Behind the misty caps of years,
> Beyond the great salt fount of tears,
> The garden lies. Strive as you may,
> You cannot miss it in your way.
> All paths that have been, or shall be,
> Pass somewhere through Gethsemane.
>
> All those who journey, soon or late,
> Must pass within the garden's gate;
> Must kneel alone in darkness there,
> And battle with some fierce despair.
> God pity those who cannot say,
> "Not mine but thine," who only pray,

"Let this cup pass," and cannot see
The *purpose* in Gethsemane.[8]

In a very real sense, God has designed a boot camp for His children, but it doesn't last just eight weeks or ten weeks. Nor is it a weekend seminar we can take or a day-long workshop we can attend. God's boot camp takes place periodically throughout the Christian life. And there, in the very center of obstacles and pain and solitude, we come to realize how alive God is in our lives—how alive and in charge. He will invade us, reduce us, break us, and crush us, so that we will become the people He intends us to be.

No matter how many years we walk with the Lord, we must still, at times, "pass somewhere through Gethsemane." It happens every time He sends us to the brook to live the hidden life. It happens every time He disorients us as He displaces us; every time He pulls out all the props; every time He takes away more of the comforts; every time He removes most of the "rights" we once enjoyed. And He does all this so that He can mold us into the person that we otherwise never would be.

Elijah went to Cherith as an energetic spokeman for God—a prophet. He emerged from Cherith as a deeper man of God. All this happened because he was "cut down to size" beside a brook that dried up.

Then the word of the LORD came to him, saying, "Arise, go to Zarephath, which belongs to Sidon, and stay there; behold, I have commanded a widow there to provide for you." So he arose and went to Zarephath, and when he came to the gate of the city, behold, a widow was there gathering sticks; and he called to her and said, "Please get me a little water in a jar, that I may drink." And as she was going to get it, he called to her and said, "Please bring me a piece of bread in your hand." But she said, "As the LORD your God lives, I have no bread, only a handful of flour in the bowl and a little oil in the jar; and behold, I am gathering a few sticks that I may go in and prepare for me and my son, that we may eat it and die." Then Elijah said to her, "Do not fear; go, do as you have said, but make me a little bread cake from it first, and bring it out to me, and afterward you may make one for yourself and for your son. For thus says the LORD God of Israel, 'The bowl of flour shall not be exhausted, nor shall the jar of oil be empty, until the day that the LORD sends rain on the face of the earth.' " So she went and did according to the word of Elijah, and she and her household ate for many days. The bowl of flour was not exhausted nor did the jar of oil become empty, according to the word of the LORD which He spoke through Elijah.

1 KINGS 17:8–16

CHAPTER THREE

Advanced Training at Zarephath

When my Marine Corps boot camp ended, I moved on to advanced infantry training. In some ways the two training regimens were alike, but the latter was even more demanding, more complicated, more rugged. Furthermore, we no longer had our ever-present drill instructor telling us every move to make. Instead of the familiar and often monotonously repetitive drills and constant harassment, we were now engaged in open-field "war games" where we practiced amphibious landings, lived out in the open, stayed awake for several days at a time, and learned to survive for extended periods of time on our own.

During those weeks of advanced training we were forced to put into action all the things we had previously discussed and studied theoretically. On top of the struggles connected with the endurance test of being without a roof over our heads, without hot meals and clean beds, we found ourselves in the presence of imaginary enemy forces against whom we were engaged in simulated battle. If captured, we would be put through severe times of deprivation and interrogation. All of this was designed to prepare us for real battle, should our country go to war.

These military-related details are more than the memories of an old Marine; I've shared them because to me they provide a dramatic analogy to what Elijah encountered during the next stage of his training as a man of God. Once he successfully made it through the rigors of Camp Cherith, an even more demanding time of advanced training awaited him at a place named Zarephath.

The dried-up brook was only the beginning. God had plans for Elijah that would take him far beyond those quiet days of isolation and meditation, where life beside the brook, with birds faithfully catering his meals, was simple, uninterrupted, and fairly routine. Anyone who would be used of God as mightily as Elijah would be in the years ahead must first face the advanced training course. For Elijah, this was Zarephath.

Because of the historical record we have in 1 Kings, we are able to watch this training transpire, and hopefully, we'll learn some valuable principles from Elijah's experiences.

> Then the word of the LORD came to him, saying, "Arise, go to Zarephath, which belongs to Sidon, and stay there; behold, I have commanded a widow there to provide for you."
>
> 1 Kings 17:8–9

As we did earlier, let's first examine the significance of the name of this place where the prophet was told to go. Zarephath comes from a Hebrew verb that means "to melt, to smelt." Interestingly, in noun form it means "crucible." The place may have gotten its name because there was a smelting plant of some kind located there; we don't know for sure. But whatever the source of its name, Zarephath would prove to be a "crucible" for Elijah—a place designed by God to further refine the prophet and make a major difference in the remainder of his life.

It was almost as if the Lord were saying to His servant, "I first took you to Cherith to wean you away from the bright lights and the public platform, where I could cut you down to size and reduce you to a man who would trust Me, regardless. It was there I began to renovate your inner man through the disciplines of solitude, silence, and obscurity. But now it's time to do an even deeper work. Now, Elijah, I will turn up the furnace and melt you so that I might mold you far more exactly into the kind of man I need to fulfill the purposes I have in mind."

If you walk with the Lord long enough, you will discover that His tests often come back-to-back. Or perhaps it would be even more accurate to say back to back to back to back to back. Usually, His preparatory tests don't stop with one or two. They multiply. And as soon as you climb out of one crucible, thinking, *Okay, I made it through that one,* you're plunged into another one, where the flame gets hotter.

Crucibles create Christlikeness. This is precisely what the hymn writer had in mind when these words were penned:

> The flame shall not hurt thee; I only design,
> Thy dross to consume and thy gold to refine.[1]

That's what a crucible does. That's what a furnace does. It brings all the impurities to the surface so that they can be skimmed off, leaving greater purity.

After I graduated from high school, I worked in a machine shop for over four years. Part of my on-the-job training took place in what was called the heat-treating department. There, three-to-four-foot bars of metal as thick as my arm were placed in the white-hot blast furnaces, where they were heated until the slag came to the surface. (Slag is useless scum that forms on the surface of molten metal; this scum is composed of all the foreign matter that makes the metal inferior.) Once these impurities were removed, the soft, extremely hot metal was formed and reshaped on huge presses as it went through the pounding of a series of hammers; then it was heated again and dropped into vats of brine or oil. At that point, the hot metal screamed, like an animal caught in a trap would scream, as it was being altered and tempered so that it could bear the beating that it was designed to take, or provide the support that it was designed to give.

GOD'S PLAN FOR ELIJAH

God knows what the future holds for His prophet. God knows the kind of strength that Elijah will need if he is going to stand strong in the battle. God knows what kind of load His prophet must be able to bear. This is no job for a wimp. Thin-skinned softies need not apply! And so he sends Elijah to the crucible of Zarephath where all the remaining dross will be burned away.

Yet even as his servant is passing through the heat of the refiner's fire, God has not forgotten him. Remember, Elijah is "inscribed on the palms of His hands" (Isaiah 49:16).

God knows where he is. "Then the word of the LORD came to him" (1 Kings 17:8). *God knows where we are.* Sometimes we forget this. Sometimes we even feel that God has forgotten us. He hasn't. God knows exactly where we are. So when you are afflicted with those forsaken feelings, when you're on the verge of throwing a pity party, thanks to those despairing thoughts, go back to the Word of God. In the heat of the crucible, seek out passages such as Isaiah 41:10:

> "Do not fear, for I am with you;
> Do not anxiously look about you, for I am your God.
> I will strengthen you, surely I will help you,
> Surely I will uphold you with My righteous right hand."

In these and a multitude of other great promises, God says, "I know where you are." *What comfort!*

God knows where Elijah is. God is there and, thankfully, He is not silent.

And, *God knows where Elijah is going.* That's something we don't know—where we're going. And I, for one, am so glad that I don't. If right now I knew everything that faced me in the coming year, I would be scared to the point of sleeplessness. But God knows. How gracious of Him to lead us one step at a time, which is exactly what He does with Elijah.

"Arise, go to Zarephath . . . and stay there," God says to Elijah.

Just take it one step at a time. "Arise." That's not difficult to do. Without doubt, Elijah was happy to leave that dried-up brook. "Go." That's not bad either. A change of scenery would be delightful. But then, the other shoe dropped: "Stay there." Ah, that's where the rub comes.

Some of us may be willing to go through a period of transitional testing. An hour or two perhaps. Maybe even a day or two. A week or so at the most. But we sure don't want to *stay there* in that place of trial.

Do you remember God's earlier instructions to Elijah? He was to *live* by the brook. Now, God told Elijah, "Go to Zarephath and *stay* there." When God said this, Elijah was at Cherith, which was somewhere east of the Jordan. If you check a map of ancient Israel, you'll find that "Zarephath, which belongs to Sidon," was located far to the west, on the coast of the Mediterranean, at least one hundred miles from Cherith. That meant a long walk across open and unprotected land where Elijah was a wanted man. King Ahab was looking everywhere for Elijah. The king had, if you will, put out a contract on the prophet of God. So, immediately, Elijah had to trust the Lord all the way from Cherith to Zarephath.

Ahab's army was aggressively searching for Elijah. Yet God told the prophet to leave his hidden place of security in the wilderness, walk out in the open, through populated regions, in order to reach his destination. What a risk. But God knew precisely where His man was going.

Because *God had prepared a place.*

> "Arise, go to Zarephath, which belongs to Sidon, and stay there; behold, I have commanded a widow there to provide for you."
>
> 1 Kings 17:9

I can't speak for you, but I would have considered that a rather humbling bit of instruction. God did not say, "I have commanded you to go to Zarephath so that you might provide for a poor widow woman." Instead, the poor widow was going to provide for this famous prophet of the Lord who stood before the king. This is a wonderful reminder that it is often the most humbling tasks that prepare us for the higher, greater tasks.

In my first year as a student at Dallas Seminary, back in 1959, I took

Greek from Dr. Bert Siegle, a soft-spoken, godly man whom God used mightily in the lives of his students. I did not know what it was that made such an impact upon us as we sat in Dr. Siegle's classroom, but at times it was as though we had been lifted into the heavenlies. Somehow this Greek professor held us in the palm of his hand.

Dr. Siegle died before my years at seminary ended in 1963. And it was not until his funeral that I discovered *how* God had refined that man into something great.

Years before, during the Depression, our school was at times unable to pay the professors' salaries. So Bert Siegle, in order to keep teaching, served as the trash man for the school. He also worked on the maintenance crew. He willingly took on the humble tasks of dumping the students' trash and laying tile in bathrooms so that he could stay on the faculty and teach those same students. When I heard that, I realized what it had been about the man that had endeared him to us: His heart of humility had won our respect.

I don't know what God has for you or for me in the future, but the refining fire of the furnace will certainly include some humbling experiences for us. They are a necessary part of God's plan. For Elijah, it was his willingness to have a poor widow provide for his needs.

ELIJAH'S TESTS

Elijah responded to God's plan with swift obedience.

> So he arose and went to Zarephath, and when he came to the gate of the city, behold, a widow was there gathering sticks; and he called to her and said, "Please get me a little water in a jar, that I may drink."
>
> And as she was going to get it, he called to her and said, "Please bring me a piece of bread in your hand."
>
> 1 Kings 17:10–11

Upon Elijah's arrival in Zarephath, he encountered two tests.

First came the test of first impressions. Never underestimate first impressions, for they are often a test. Elijah was dying of thirst. The brook had been dried up for an undisclosed period of time. Then he had trekked a hundred miles across a dry and barren land. By the time he arrived at his destination, he was desperately in need of water. At the gate of the city of Zarephath he saw a widow gathering sticks. Aha, this must be the widow who was going to provide for him.

"Please get me a drink of water," Elijah said. "Oh, and while you're at it, could you bring me a piece of bread too?"

> But she said, "As the LORD your God lives, I have no bread, only a handful of flour in the bowl and a little oil in the jar; and behold, I am gathering a few sticks that I may go in and prepare for me and my son, that we may eat it and die."
>
> 1 Kings 17:12

What a surprise! Welcome to Zarephath, Elijah! This was the person who was supposed to provide for him?

Elijah went to Zarephath anticipating at least a little more provision than he'd had at Cherith. Yet those first impressions would suggest otherwise. Apparently he was going to get even less. Perhaps he wouldn't die of thirst, but it looked as if he might starve to death.

Have you ever been blindsided by first impressions? Have you ever made plans for going to a new school or a new church? Or moving to a new town to take a new job? Or taking on new challenges? Then, suddenly, it's different than you had planned. But it's not only different . . . *it's worse.* This is what I call the first-impression blues. They can be terrible!

In the summer of 1961 I did a pastoral internship at Peninsula Bible Church at Palo Alto, California. At the end of the summer when Pastor Ray Stedman and I sat down to evaluate my time there, I said to him rather bluntly, "You know, when we first came back in May, it was really a letdown, Ray. It was a Saturday night, after dark. You were gone. The church staff was gone. There was nobody here to meet us. I didn't know where we were supposed to go or what we were supposed to do. I had to make two or three phone calls before I could reach anyone who could help us. It was really discouraging."

Ray just smiled and said, "Chuck, that was all part of the training."

"I don't remember reading that in the manual anywhere," I said.

"No," said Ray, "you didn't." Then he added a few words of counsel I remember to this day. "But, Chuck, you're going to find all the way through your life and ministry that you'll come up against the problem of beginning something—and when you do, you will immediately encounter the difficulties involved. The way you handled that Saturday night disappointment told us something about the mettle of your character," which, I might add, was rather soft and thin-skinned at that point. I needed that testing and that counsel, and it has served me well.

Elijah came to Zarephath and found nothing but a woman looking for sticks so that she could build a fire, fix her last meal, and die of starvation. What a letdown after his long and arduous journey.

That brings up the second test—*the test of physical impossibilities*. Elijah had walked into a situation that was, from all human perspective, impossible. But the good news is that he saw beyond the difficulty. He handled the problem with faith, not fear. Look at what he did.

> Then Elijah said to her, "Do not fear; go, do as you have said, but make me a little bread cake from it first, and bring it out to me, and afterward you may make one for yourself and for your son.
>
> "For thus says the LORD God of Israel, 'The bowl of flour shall not be exhausted, nor shall the jar of oil be empty, until the day that the LORD sends rain on the face of the earth.' "
>
> 1 Kings 17:13–14

Elijah was determined that those initial first-impression blues were not going to get him down. The widow had her eyes on the impossibilities: a handful of flour, a tiny amount of oil, a few sticks. Elijah rolled up his sleeves and focused only on the possibilities.

How could he do that? Because he was an emerging man of God.

He had been to Cherith. He had seen the proof of God's faithfulness. He had survived the dried-up brook. He had obeyed God and, without hesitation, he had walked to Zarephath.

You can't talk the talk if you've never walked the walk. You can't encourage somebody else to believe the improbable if you haven't believed the impossible. You can't light another's candle of hope if your own torch of faith isn't burning.

When Elijah saw the near-empty flour bin and oil jug, he said, almost with a shrug, "That's no problem for God. Get in there and fix those biscuits. And fix some for you and your son, too." Then he told her why. Listen to these confident words of faith: "The bowl of flour shall not be exhausted, nor the jar of oil be empty, until the day that the Lord sends rain on the face of this earth."

What a promise! That woman must have looked at Elijah, this tired dusty stranger, with wonder and bewilderment, as she heard words like she'd never heard before.

Have you ever spent time in the presence of a person of faith? Ever rubbed shoulders with men and women of God who don't have the word "impossible" in their vocabulary? If not, locate a few strong-hearted souls. You need them in your life. These are the kind of incredible associations God uses to build up *our* faith!

That widow at the gates of Zarephath listened to Elijah with her mouth wide open, and, I'm convinced, she was never the same again. Elijah modeled for her the lesson he had already learned himself: the lesson of faithful obedience. God told him "go" and he went. Now, Elijah tells the woman to practice the same kind of obedience. He tells her to "go" and "do."

> So she *went* and *did* according to the word of Elijah, and she and he and her household ate for many days.
>
> The bowl of flour was not exhausted nor did the jar of oil become empty, according to the word of the LORD which He spoke through Elijah.
>
> 1 Kings 17:15–16 (italics added)

In response, "she went" and "she did." That's obedience in its simplest form.

Man's obedience and God's faithfulness—that's a combination that leads to miracles! Read it again and again. In the midst of the crucible, Elijah and the widow obeyed, and God provided a miracle. The bowl of flour was never empty. The jar of oil was never dry. How thrilling it must have been for that woman and her son to sit down at the table and eat those miracle biscuits.

The widow of Zarephath met God in the kitchen. She looked into the bowl and she found flour. She looked in the jar and she found oil. The last time she had checked the pantry, there was barely enough for a small portion. Now, morning and evening, day in and day out, she gave God praise for His provision. I can almost hear that ancient doxology flowing from her lips as she prepared those daily meals: "Praise God from whom all biscuits flow. . . ."

Now, this doesn't mean that the woman and her son had everything they wanted. But it does mean they had all they needed. When you've come to the end of your own resources, and God says no to your wants but yes to your needs, you are more than satisfied.

After studying what followed in the prophet's life, I believe this was a crossroads in Elijah's preparation as a man of God.

FOUR LESSONS . . . PRINCIPLES WORTH PONDERING

As I look at this turning point in Elijah's life and ministry, I also find four lingering lessons for our lives.

Number one: God's leading is often surprising; don't analyze it. If God leads you to Zarephath, don't try to make sense out of it. Just go. If God places you in a difficult situation, and you have peace that you are to stay there, don't analyze it or run away from it. Stay put. The longer I live, the more I believe that God's leading is often humanly illogical. It's a mystery, at least from our limited perspective.

Number Two: The beginning days are often the hardest days; don't quit. Remember my earlier comments about those first-impression blues? They are real. And they can cause us to panic and toss in the towel. Don't. The adversary of our souls loves to derail us, discourage us, and tempt us to quit altogether. Let's learn from Elijah's example. Not even a poor widow, who hardly had enough energy to gather a few sticks of firewood to cook her last meal, discouraged him. And God used his faith to ignite new hope in her and provide a reason to go on. Confidence in God is contagious.

Number Three: God's promises often hinge on obedience; don't ignore your part. "Elijah, arise and go," God said. So Elijah arose and went. "Woman, go in there and fix the meal," said Elijah. So she went and fixed the meal. A promise fulfilled is often the result of our obedience. When promises have conditions, our obedience precedes God's provision. Be careful about any teaching that leads to passivity. Resting in the Lord is one thing; passive indifference is something else entirely.

Number Four: God's provisions are often just enough; don't fail to thank Him. Maybe you don't have the job you wanted, but you do have a job. Maybe you don't have the position you planned on, but His provisions are enough . . . just enough. If you postpone your gratitude until all your dreams are fulfilled, you could easily turn into a cranky Christian, always waiting for more. Grateful contentment is a much-needed virtue in this consumptive culture.

> Being determined to perfect His saints, [God] puts His precious metal into His crucible. But He sits by it, and watches it. Love is His thermometer, and marks the exact degree of heat; not one instant's unnecessary pang will He permit; and as soon as the dross is released so that He sees Himself reflected in the fire, the trial ceases.[2]

As soon as the Lord sees His image in you, the furnace cools and you are ready for the next series of events He has planned for you.

The Son of God, our Savior, faced the ultimate test, the fiercest fire, when He went to the cross. He didn't fight the will of God; He accepted it. He said, "I came to do Your will, O God." And aren't we grateful that He didn't quit, that He didn't turn back? He followed through to the very end. That's why we exult in His *finished* work at Calvary!

The next time you sing these lines, remember Elijah's advanced training at Zarephath:

> The flame shall not hurt thee; I only design,
> Thy dross to consume and thy gold to refine.[3]

It is not only possible but also probable that most of us have gone through the crucible at some time in our life, or we will at some point ahead. We've been to Cherith and we've walked to Zarephath. It's all part of God's plan. Never forget, Jesus Christ was "a man of sorrows and acquainted with grief" (Isaiah 53:3). We can never be like Him without enduring the crucible.

On the Christian journey from faith to maturity, all roads pass through Zarephath.

Now it came about after these things, that the son of the woman, the mistress of the house, became sick; and his sickness was so severe, that there was no breath left in him. So she said to Elijah, "What do I have to do with you, O man of God? You have come to me to bring my iniquity to remembrance, and to put my son to death!" And he said to her, "Give me your son." Then he took him from her bosom and carried him up to the upper room where he was living, and laid him on his own bed. And he called to the LORD and said, "O LORD my God, hast Thou also brought calamity to the widow with whom I am staying, by causing her son to die?" Then he stretched himself upon the child three times, and called to the LORD, and said, "O LORD my God, I pray Thee, let this child's life return to him." And the LORD heard the voice of Elijah, and the life of the child returned to him and he revived. And Elijah took the child, and brought him down from the upper room into the house and gave him to his mother; and Elijah said, "See, your son is alive." Then the woman said to Elijah, "Now I know that you are a man of God, and that the word of the LORD in your mouth is truth."

1 KINGS 17:17–24

CHAPTER FOUR

Standing in the Shadow of God

Hebrews 11 is like a *Reader's Digest* condensed version of the men and women of faith in the Old Testament. This chapter gives us their names and tells us, briefly, what they accomplished . . . "by faith." This invaluable record not only opens our own eyes of faith, challenging us to walk as they walked, but also gives us dramatic insights into the remarkable ways of God.

- "By faith Abel offered to God a better sacrifice."
- "By faith Enoch was taken up so that he should not see death."
- "By faith Noah, being warned by God about things not yet seen, in reverence prepared an ark."
- "By faith Abraham, when he was called, obeyed."
- "By faith even Sarah herself received ability to conceive."
- "By faith Isaac blessed Jacob and Esau."
- "By faith Jacob, as he was dying, blessed each of the sons of Joseph."
- "By faith Joseph, when he was dying, made mention of the exodus."
- "By faith Moses, when he was born, was hidden for three months by his parents."

- "By faith Moses, when he had grown up, refused to be called the son of Pharaoh's daughter."
- "By faith Rahab the harlot did not perish along with those who were disobedient."

After this wonderful roll call of faithful men and women, we come to a startling statement: "Women received back their dead by resurrection" (Hebrews 11:35).

I find it interesting that Elijah is not included in God's "hall of faith." Even though Elijah's was a life characterized by one act of faith after another, God chose not to mention him, at least by name. Yet when we come to this statement—"women received back their dead by resurrection"—I am convinced the Lord did have Elijah's faith in mind, for one of those returns to life happened in Elijah's day and on his watch. It was God who brought about this miracle, using His prophet and servant Elijah.

As this roll call of faith attests, God specializes in impossible situations. On at least four separate occasions in the Scriptures we are told that He does what we cannot do: He specializes in impossibilities.

"'Ah Lord God! Behold, Thou hast made the heavens and the earth by Thy great power and by Thine outstretched arm! Nothing is too difficult for Thee.'"

Jeremiah 32:17

"Behold, I am the Lord, the God of all flesh; is anything too difficult for Me?"

Jeremiah 32:27

"For nothing will be impossible with God."

Luke 1:37

But He said, "The things impossible with men are possible with God."

Luke 18:27

There are times when God acts completely on His own to accomplish the impossible. When He created the world, there was no one but God. When He raised Christ from the dead, there was no one but God. He acted alone.

But more often than not, God uses others in the process. In the list we read earlier, numerous individuals engaged in miraculous exploits, though, clearly, the power to accomplish those exploits came from God. He could have worked on His own in every case, yet He deliberately worked His miracles through human instruments—through people just like us, who (unlike God) could never have done the impossible, but who (through God) were engaged in the miracle. They were on the scene when the Lord chose to do what humans cannot do on their own. Through their words or hands or activities He accomplished the impossible.

While standing in the shadow of God, they became instruments of His miraculous power. That's exactly where we find Elijah in an event recorded in 1 Kings 17.

GO AWAY AND HIDE

> Now it came about after these things, that the son of the woman, the mistress of the house, became sick; and his sickness was so severe, that there was no breath left in him.
>
> 1 Kings 17:17

The first question that comes to mind as I read this opening line of the story is "After what things?" What were the circumstances that led up to this moment for Elijah? Remember with me as I rehearse the previous events.

First, God gave Elijah the courage to confront Ahab and announce a drought. Following closely on the heels of that announcement, God told Elijah to do an incredible thing: He was not to stay before the public; instead, he was to run and hide by the brook Cherith. While there, he was to be fed by the ravens twice a day, and he was to draw his water from the brook—which later dried up. At Cherith, for an undisclosed period of time, Elijah simply waited upon God in the solitude of obscurity. In the process he became a man of God. He learned to lean on his Lord.

Next, God sent Elijah to Zarephath. He was to go from the *cutting down* and the brokenness of Cherith to the furnace-like *crucible* of refinement. When he got there, he found a widow and her child on the verge of starvation. At God's direction, Elijah moved in with them. Elijah said to the widow, in effect, "We will trust God on a day-by-day basis." And, sure enough, God came through day after day (as He always does). The flour bin was never empty, and the little jar of oil never ran dry. Each and every day God provided for their needs.

And thus it was that in this context of hiding and testing, "after these things," Elijah faced another impossible situation. But there is a difference. By now, Elijah has become accustomed to facing the impossible. His faith has matured. He's ready for the next test, confident in His God.

A DEATH IN THE FAMILY

> Now it came about after these things, that the son of the woman, the
> mistress of the house, became sick; and his sickness was so severe, that
> there was no breath left in him.
>
> 1 Kings 17:17

We are not told what was wrong with the widow's son, but the illness was so severe that the boy died. He had "no breath left in him." And when that happened, his mother looked around for someone to blame. That's a natural reaction. It is human nature to want to blame someone for the bad things that happen in life. This is often true when sudden death takes a loved one. Sometimes we even blame those who have done the most to help.

> So she said to Elijah, "What do I have to do with you, O man of God?
> You have come to me to bring my iniquity to remembrance, and to
> put my son to death!"
>
> 1 Kings 17:18

The woman blames Elijah for the worst thing that has ever happened to her: the death of her beloved son. She also looks upon the death as a condemnation from the hand of God. Even though the prophet had done nothing to deserve her reaction, even though she and her son had been sustained through the miraculous provision of food each day, thanks to the presence of Elijah and the power of his God, she blamed him.

But let's not judge her too severely. Those who have lost a loved one, especially a child, understand her grief. Sometimes in situations like that we say things we later regret. So we understand what this bereaved mother might have been thinking and feeling when she looked at Elijah and said, "O man of God, what have you done to me? Have you come to punish my sins by killing my son?" (NLT).

She stands there, tears streaming down her face, holding the body of her son in her arms. And at that precise moment Elijah holds out *his* arms and says, "Give him to me."

> And he said to her, "Give me your son." Then he took him from her bosom and carried him up to the upper room where he was living, and laid him on his own bed.
>
> 1 Kings 17:19

There the woman stands, holding the limp, lifeless body of her only child. Her world has come crashing down, suddenly and unexpectedly. And Elijah simply says, "Give him to me."

Do you know what really impresses me here? It's the silence of Elijah. Somehow he knows that nothing he can say at this moment will satisfy this grieving mother. No words from him can soothe her stricken spirit. So he does not argue with her. He does not rebuke her. He does not try to reason with her. He doesn't remind her of all she owes him or of how ashamed she should be for blaming him. He simply asks her to place her burden in his arms.

Pause for a moment to realize that Elijah is again in a situation that, at least from a human point of view, he doesn't deserve. He has obeyed God by going to Ahab then hiding at Cherith. He has walked with God from Cherith to Zarephath. He has done *exactly* as the Lord instructed. He's trusted God, and now he's receiving the brunt of this woman's blame.

God sometimes seems to put us in the vise, and then He tightens it and tightens it more, until we think, in the pain of His sovereign squeeze, "What's He trying to do to me?" We walk closer to Him and even closer to Him. We don't see how we could walk any closer, but still more tests come, one on top of another.

That's where Elijah is, but he doesn't waver. He stands tall and silent in the shadow of God, grounded in faith, confident of his Lord's power. That's humility at its best.

He doesn't question God. He doesn't fall apart at the seams. He doesn't lose control. He doesn't argue with the woman. He simply says, with quiet compassion, "Give me the boy."

I'm also deeply impressed by the man's gentleness. Though Elijah deserved none of the woman's blame, he stood silent under her blast. That's gentleness. Someone, somewhere, has called this fruit of the Spirit "the mint-mark of heaven." When it is present in a highly charged setting such as this, it becomes a testimony of the Spirit of God at work in the one who could lash back, but doesn't. It is His life, at that gentle and tender moment, being made evident.

Many years ago my mother taught me a little piece that I often quote to myself to this day. When I am tempted to be defensive and am provoked to retaliate verbally, these lines occasionally come to my rescue.

> Gentle Spirit, dwell with me,
> I myself would gentle be;
> And with words that help and heal,
> Would Thy like in mine reveal.[1]

I am also impressed with this grieving mother. She, without question or hesitation, places her precious, lifeless son into Elijah's arms. Perhaps the prophet's gentleness suddenly melted her and prompted her, once again, to trust him.

Then, Elijah, the man of God, silently climbed the stairway to the room where he had been doing battle before God on a regular basis. I say this because I believe that Elijah had spent hours, even days, on his knees in that room. He had formed that habit while alone with his God at Cherith.

Do you have a room like that—a place where you meet with God? Do you have a quiet retreat where you and the Lord do regular business together? If you don't, I strongly urge you to provide yourself just such a place—your own prophet's chamber where you and God can meet together. It will be there that you will prepare yourself for life's contingencies. Without it, you'll lack the necessary steel in the foundation of your faith.

What do you do when tragedy strikes? What do you do when a test comes? What's your first response? Is it to complain? To blame? To try to reason your way out of it? Or have you formed the habit of doing what Elijah did? Do you go to your special place and get alone with God? Elijah provides a wonderful example for us. No panic. No fear. No rush. No doubt. Why should he? For he knows that . . .

> He who dwells in the shelter of the Most High
> Will abide in the shadow of the Almighty.
> I will say to the LORD, "My refuge and my fortress,
> My God, in whom I trust!"
> For it is He who delivers you from the snare of the trapper,
> And from the deadly pestilence.
> He will cover you with His pinions,
> And under His wings you may seek refuge;
> His faithfulness is a shield and bulwark.
>
> Psalm 91:1–4

ALONE WITH GOD

Now, let's walk slowly through these next few moments as we witness Elijah standing in the shadow of the Almighty. It's a sacred scene. Let's treat it as such.

First, Elijah tenderly places the body of the boy on his bed and then goes before God in prayer.

> And he called to the LORD and said, "O LORD my God, hast Thou also brought calamity to the widow with whom I am staying, by causing her son to die?"
>
> 1 Kings 17:20

Elijah may have been silent before the woman, but not before God. It is before God that he raises his tough questions.

"Lord, what are You doing? What are You trying to tell me? Why would You break the heart of this dear mother? I've obeyed You. I've waited upon You. I've urged her to wait upon You. And now this? This situation is beyond me; I can't seem to get above it. I can't get relief from it. Lord, what are You doing? What do You *mean* by this?"

All alone in the shadow of God . . . that's where we fight such battles. Elijah is able to be completely candid with his God because he's developed such familiarity over time in his own private place of struggle—in his own spiritual haven.

> Then he stretched himself upon the child three times, and called to the LORD, and said, "O LORD my God, I pray Thee, let this child's life return to him."
>
> 1 Kings 17:21

Now wait a minute. What is going on here? Up to this point in Scripture there has been no account of anyone ever being raised from the dead. The closest to that would be Enoch, but he was not resurrected or resuscitated, because he didn't die. God simply took him to glory. "And Enoch walked with God; and he was not, for God took him" (Genesis 5:24).

So what is Elijah thinking here? How does he dare ask God to do such an unprecedented thing?

Elijah could not go back through the record like some spiritual attorney and try to find another case he could point to and say, "Ah! Precedence recorded in the Scriptures—there's a case like mine. God did it there. He will do it here." But God never claimed to provide a written record of *absolutely everything* He has ever done. And I believe He has left the record incomplete, so to speak, so that we will not trust in the past but in the God who is fresh and alive and creative and real, able to meet today's need *today*.

Elijah had no this-is-how-God-always-does-it manual to follow. Instead, he relied solely on one thing: faith. He had only his faith in the living God.

Don't you wish at times that you had a book where you could look up "impatience"? Okay. "What to do when I'm impatient in the face of testing":

here are steps one, two, three, four, and five. And in case of severe emergency: six, seven, and eight. You've got the answer! Or, what to do when death comes: one, two, three, four. If it is the dearest friend you've ever known: five and six. If it is your own child: seven and eight. But there's no such manual. Thankfully, in His Word God does include principles to follow in most crises, but not a precise procedure in all difficult or impossible situations. God leaves us on the cutting edge of today so that we will trust in Him and the principles in His great and gracious Word. That's all we have.

So, trusting in the living God, Elijah literally spread himself across the body of the dead boy. Ceremonially, that was an unclean act, because a man of God was not to touch the dead. But this impossible situation called for an extreme exception. Therefore, Elijah got on the bed and laid himself on the body of that boy—leg to leg, arm to arm, face to face. "He stretched himself upon the child three times."

I don't know why he employed such an unusual method, nor why he did it three times. Perhaps, in the process of talking to the Lord, he had received an indication that this was what he was supposed to do. And apparently he did not quit until he received the assurance from God that it was time to stop . . . and leave it with Him.

> Then he stretched himself upon the child three times, and called to the Lord, and said, "O Lord my God, I pray Thee, let this child's life return to him."
>
> 1 Kings 17:21

That was some prayer. Elijah was not able to say, "Let this child's life return to him, as it happened to Enoch, as it happened to Isaac, as it happened to Moses," because there was no precedence for this particular miracle. So Elijah said, "Lord, I'm trusting You for a miracle. I'm asking You to perform the impossible." He then waited. Everything, at that epochal moment of faith, rested in the Lord's hands.

Some of you may be in the process of placing your own life before the Lord in this way. Things are critical, and only a miracle can breathe new life into your situation. Circumstances are totally out of your control. So you take it to your special place and, standing in the shadow of your God, you lay it out before Him, prostrating yourself before Him, pleading for His intervention, trusting completely in His miraculous power, leaning not on your own understanding.

Dr. Raymond Edman, in his little book, *In Quietness and Confidence*, writes about a godly man who faced just such a trial.

> This is how he met it: He was quiet for a while with his Lord, then he wrote these words for himself:
>
> First, He brought me here, it is by His will I am in this strait place: in that fact I will rest.
>
> Next, He will keep me here in His love, and give me grace to behave as His child.
>
> Then, He will make the trial a blessing, teaching me the lessons He intends me to learn, and working in me the grace He means to bestow.
>
> Last, in His time He can bring me out again—how and when He knows.[2]

Can you make these four statements? If you can ... *will* you?

1. I am here by God's appointment.
2. I am in His keeping.
3. I am under His training.
4. He will show me His purposes in His time.

By God's appointment, in God's keeping, under His training, for His time. What an outstanding summary of what it means to trust in the Lord with *all* your heart!

Elijah said, "Lord, I am here by Your appointment. This is no accident. I am standing under Your shadow. This is Your call. And in Your time, I ask You to do not only the incredible but the impossible."

> And the LORD heard the voice of Elijah, and the life of the child returned to him and he revived.
>
> 1 Kings 17:22

No words can describe what happened in that little upstairs bedroom when the corpse began to stir and Elijah saw life come back into the boy's body. No words can describe being in the midst of such a trial and then watching God, in a miraculous moment or period of time, work it out. Only you who have been there can nod, smile, and say, "Amen. I know exactly what you're saying. I've seen God do it."

Elijah saw that kind of miracle. It happened before his eyes.

Now, look at what he did.

> And Elijah took the child, and brought him down from the upper room into the house and gave him to his mother; and Elijah said, "See, your son is alive."
>
> 1 Kings 17:23

Elijah did not say, "See what I did!" No! That's what *we* might have done, or perhaps that's what some televangelist might do . . . but that's not what Elijah did. Elijah simply walked downstairs with the boy by his side and said, "See, your son is alive."

Once again, words fail to describe the feelings of the mother, or the experience between mother and child at that moment.

In years past, Cynthia and I had a close, personal friend who was a dear woman of God and therefore a faithful woman of prayer. She prayed for us for many years. Periodically she would ask, "What's the Lord doing in your life?" When we told her about various things that were happening, her response invariably was, "Isn't that just like the Lord." Or, "Isn't the Lord wonderful! That's just like Him to do this." Rather than being surprised, she was always humbly affirming and grateful. Her God never disappointed. His miraculous powers only strengthened her faith . . . and ours!

Now, that's what Elijah wanted this woman to see. He stepped back into the shadows so that she would see the Lord.

Elijah wanted her to see what God had done and be impressed with Him, not His servant. And look at the results!

> Then the woman said to Elijah, "Now I know that you are a man of God, and that the word of the LORD in your mouth is truth."
>
> 1 Kings 17:24

When the woman saw that her son was alive, she didn't see Elijah. She saw the Lord.

"Elijah, I've heard you talk about the God of heaven. I've heard you refer to Him in various ways. But now when I look at this miracle, I know that you speak the truth."

FAITH PERSONIFIED

In the Gospel of Luke, Jesus exhorts those who wish to be people of God:

> For each tree is known by its own fruit. For men do not gather figs from thorns, nor do they pick grapes from a briar bush. The good man out of the good treasure of his heart brings forth what is good; and the evil man out of the evil treasure brings forth what is evil; for his mouth speaks from that which fills his heart.
>
> And why do you call Me, "Lord, Lord," and do not do what I say?
>
> Everyone who comes to Me, and hears My words, and acts upon them, I will show you whom he is like: he is like a man building a house, who dug deep and laid a foundation upon the rock; and when a flood rose, the torrent burst against that house and could not shake it, because it had been well built.
>
> Luke 6:44–48

If you wish to be a man or woman of God, it is essential that you face the impossible situations of life with faith, as Elijah did. If you are a young person who desires to live a godly life that will leave its mark upon this world, you must stand in the shadow of your Savior, trusting Him to work through the trials you encounter, through the extreme circumstances you cannot handle on your own. The God of Elijah is your God, and He is still the God of impossible situations. He still does what no earthly individual can do.

Elijah approached the impossible with calmness and contentment, with gentleness and self-control, with faith and humility. As I've mentioned from the beginning, Elijah was heroic in exploits of faith, but he was always a model of humility.

Examine your own life for these character traits and take them one by one before God. You might say to the Lord, for example, "Lord, today I want to do what You say regarding contentment; I want to have a calm and gentle spirit. I don't simply want to call myself a Christian. I want to be known as a genuine servant of God because my life demonstrates the truth I say I believe. Help me this day to face everything and deal with everyone with a gentle and quiet spirit. Help me to be content, even though I don't get things my way.

"Help me today with diligence, Lord. I tend to lose sight of the goal as the day wears on. I'm a good starter, but I don't finish well. Help me to do a quality piece of work and not to give in to the mood of the moment.

"And, Lord, help me, when You begin to bring to pass these qualities in my life, not to display them, but just to let them flow out in glory to You. Help me to become Your servant, Your man, Your woman."

That is how we personify a life of faith.

All over this world, around us every day, are people who are looking for the truth to be lived out in the lives of those who claim it. Just as the widow watched Elijah, there are people watching you. They hear what you say you believe, but mainly they are watching to see what you do.

Remember, you are here by God's appointment, you are in His keeping, you are under His training, for His time. Give Him the corpse of your life, and ask Him to revive those lifeless areas that need to be revived. If the situation calls for it, trust Him for a miracle, in His time, if it be His will, for your life.

On the bed of your life place the remains of your broken and scarred past . . . the emptiness of your poor character traits . . . the habits that have so long controlled you . . . the limited vision that continues to characterize you . . . the slight irritation that nags or the large one that looms . . . the anger or violence or lust or greed or discontentment or selfishness or the ugliness of pride. Lay these things before the Father and stretch yourself out under His shadow as you ask Him to bring about remarkable, even miraculous changes in your life.

Is He able? Get serious! I'm referring to "the God of impossibilities," the One who has limitless power, who has never—and *will* never—meet an intimidating obstacle He cannot overcome, an aggressive enemy He cannot overwhelm, a final decision He cannot override, or a powerful person He cannot overshadow.

Because Elijah believed in "the God of impossibilities," not even death caused him to doubt. He learned his theology of faith in the secret hiding place at Cherith. He was given the opportunity to develop it during his advance training at Zarephath. But it was not until he stared death in the face, literally, that he personified it. And he did it all standing in the shadow of God.

And so must I.

And so must you.

Now it happened after many days, that the word of the LORD came to Elijah in the third year, saying, "Go, show yourself to Ahab, and I will send rain on the face of the earth." So Elijah went to show himself to Ahab. . . . And it came about, when Ahab saw Elijah that Ahab said to him, "Is this you, you troubler of Israel?" And he said, "I have not troubled Israel, but you and your father's house have, because you have forsaken the commandments of the LORD, and you have followed the Baals. Now then send and gather to me all Israel at Mount Carmel, together with 450 prophets of Baal and 400 prophets of the Asherah, who eat at Jezebel's table." So Ahab sent a message among all the sons of Israel, and brought the prophets together at Mount Carmel. And Elijah came near to all the people and said, "How long will you hesitate between two opinions? If the LORD is God, follow Him; but if Baal, follow him." But the people did not answer him a word. Then Elijah said to the people, "I alone am left a prophet of the LORD, but Baal's prophets are 450 men. Now let them give us two oxen; and let them choose one ox for themselves and cut it up, and place it on the wood, but put no fire under it; and I will prepare the other ox, and lay it on the wood, and I will not put a fire under it. Then you call on the name of your god, and I will call on the name of the LORD, and the God who answers by fire, He is God." And all the people answered and said, "That is a good idea." So Elijah said to the prophets of Baal, "Choose one ox for yourselves and prepare it first for you are many, and call on the name of your god, but put no fire under it." Then they took the ox which was given them and they prepared it and called on the name of Baal from morning until noon saying, "O Baal, answer us." But there was no voice and no one answered. And they leaped about the altar which they made. And it came about at noon, that Elijah mocked them and said, "Call out with a loud voice, for he is a god; either he is occupied or gone aside, or is on a journey, or perhaps he is asleep and needs to be awakened." So they cried with a loud voice and cut themselves according to their custom with swords and lances until the blood gushed out on them. And it came about when midday was past, that they raved until the time of the offering of the eventing sacrifice; but there was no voice, no one answered, and no one paid attention. Then Elijah said to all the people, "Come near to me." So all the people came near to him. And he repaired the altar of the LORD which had been torn down. And Elijah took twelve stones according to the number of the tribes of the sons of Jacob, to whom the word of the LORD had come, saying, "Israel shall be your name." So with the stones he built an altar in the name of the LORD, and he made a trench around the altar, large enough to hold two measures of seed. Then he arranged the wood and cut the ox in pieces and laid it on the wood. And he said, "Fill four pitchers with water and pour it on the burnt offering and on the wood." And he said, "Do it a second time," and they did it a second time. And he said, "Do it a third time," and they did it a third time. And the water flowed around the altar, and he also filled the trench with water. Then it came about at the time of the offering of the evening sacrifice, that Elijah the prophet came near and said, "O LORD, the God of Abraham, Isaac and Israel, today let it be known that Thou art God in Israel, and that I am Thy servant, and that I have done all these things at Thy word. "Answer me, O LORD, answer me, that this people may know that Thou, O LORD, art God, and that Thou hast turned their heart back again." Then the fire of the LORD fell, and consumed the burnt offering and the wood and the stones and the dust, and licked up the water that was in the trench. And when all the people saw it, they fell on their faces; and they said, "The LORD, He is God; the LORD, He is God." Then Elijah said to them, "Seize the prophets of Baal; do not let one of them escape." So they seized them; and Elijah brought them down to the brook Kishon, and slew them there.

1 KINGS 18:1–2, 17–40

CHAPTER FIVE

The God Who Answers by Fire

Having just stepped into a new millennium as well as a new century, we have been bombarded with lists from the previous century. The greatest people. The greatest discoveries. The most important inventions. The best athletes. The best film actors. The most influential philosophers. The worst disasters. Again and again, during the countdown to January 1, 2000, our television screens, newspapers and magazines presented us with lists of people and events that made history, that set world records, that permanently etched themselves into the chronicles of time. Some amazing things occurred in the twentieth century!

Given this precedent, if *Time, Newsweek,* and *People* magazines had been around at the turn of the century in 700 B.C., would they have included Elijah on one of their lists, if only for one major event in his life? I don't see how anyone summing up the people and events of the previous one hundred years could have ignored this significant showdown—this classic "fight to the finish" between the pagan gods of the earth and the living God in the heavens. Imagine the headlines:

"The Battle of the Gods"

or
"The Greatest Conflict of the Century"
or even
"The God Who Answers by Fire"

Today, in the land of Israel, an oversized statue of Elijah stands on a high pedestal at the peak of Mount Carmel. I've stopped to look at it during every trip I've made to the Holy Land. There stands the bearded prophet Elijah, with a large knife held in his hand, raised high above his head. Below is an inscription that refers to this unforgettable conflict. For somewhere near the summit of that very mountain, the prophet of God stood toe to toe with the prophets of Baal, calling down a dramatic, fiery proof of which one was the true and only deity, deserving of human worship and worthy of devoted obedience.

Before we come to that moment, though, let's look at a few of the events that led up to it. You'll recall that in 1 Kings 17:1, God sent His prophet Elijah to King Ahab to announce that "There shall be neither dew nor rain these years, except by My word." Then God told Elijah to "Go away from here and turn eastward, and hide yourself by the brook Cherith" (17:3). After God's purposes for His prophet had been completed at Cherith, He sent him on to Zarephath. In both places, Elijah had to trust God completely for his food and drink; and God never failed to provide them—in ways Elijah could never have imagined.

Months, then years passed. As the earth dried up, Ahab scoured Israel and the surrounding nations, looking for Elijah, but the prophet could not be found. Meanwhile, Elijah was waiting, trusting by faith, that God would show him the next step.

AFTER THREE YEARS!

Now it came about after many days, that the word of the LORD came to Elijah in the third year, saying, "Go, show yourself to Ahab, and I will send rain on the face of the earth."

1 Kings 18:1

Finally, after three long years, God speaks to His servant and says, "Go, show yourself to Ahab." Three years earlier God had said, "Go, hide yourself." Now He says, "Go, show yourself." Three years earlier God had said, "There is going to be a drought in the land. There will be neither rain nor dew until I say so." Now He says, "I will send rain."

The encounter between Elijah and Ahab must have been something to behold. Remember, Elijah was the most wanted man in the land. King Ahab had sent his minions searching high and low for the prophet.

> So Elijah went to show himself to Ahab. Now the famine was severe in Samaria. . . . And it came about, when Ahab saw Elijah that Ahab said to him, "Is this you, you troubler of Israel?"
>
> 1 Kings 28:2, 17

The noun form of the Hebrew verb that means "to trouble, to bring calamity" is here translated *troubler*. There are occasions when this Hebrew word is used to mean "viper, asp, or snake." So "troubler" is another way of saying, "Is that you, you sorry snake in the grass?" In other words, Ahab leaves no doubt about how he feels about Elijah. To him, the prophet is a snake. He's behind all the trouble in the land. And there was plenty of trouble, to be sure.

Try to imagine the scene: Three years without a drop of rain in the entire land of Israel. Every brook had dried up. When Elijah made his way from Zarephath to Ahab's palace, he must have walked around the carcasses and skeletons of many a beast. Imagine what the stench of death must have been like. To help you picture the scene, just recall the evening news reports of the devastating toll of drought and famine in sections of Africa— the pictures of disease and death everywhere across vast regions.

Now, into the midst of this terrible scene walks the man who is being blamed for it all: Elijah.

King Ahab meets the prophet with fire in his eyes, spitting out his condemnation: "You troubler of Israel. You sneaky snake."

Think about the courage that it took for Elijah to go to Ahab. Think about the faith it took for him to walk into this scene. Yet, having been trained at Cherith and further prepared at Zarephath, Elijah was not intimidated. Not in the least. On the contrary, he had the audacity to shift the blame back where it belonged.

> And he said, "I have not troubled Israel, but you and your father's house have, because you have forsaken the commandments of the LORD, and you have followed the Baals."
>
> 1 Kings 18:18

"Don't blame *me* for what's happened," Elijah tells Ahab boldly. "God brought this drought of judgment because of people like *you*. You're the reason we haven't had rain. God has restrained the heavens because you have broken His commandments. You have forsaken Him. You are worshiping idols." Elijah didn't back down one inch.

Elijah's message was severe because Ahab had been so shamelessly disobedient. The monarch had brazenly broken the very first commandment, "You shall have no other gods before me" (Exodus 20:3). Ahab needed to know that the God of heaven is supreme, and Elijah was ready to prove it. And thus the showdown began: Ahab vs. Elijah. No, actually, it was a dramatic showdown between idolatry and the living God.

PREPARATION FOR THE PROOF

Elijah begins by offering a plan. But before we discuss that plan, let's take a quick look at the audience Elijah assembled.

> Now then send and gather to me all Israel at Mount Carmel, together with 450 prophets of Baal and 400 prophets of the Asherah, who eat at Jezebel's table.
>
> 1 Kings 18:19

Elijah not only boldly rebukes the king of the land, he also orders him to assemble all the prophets of Baal and Asherah, the prominent deities of the day in Israel. We can see how prominent they were by the number of idolatrous prophets they had, as well as their exalted position in the kingdom. According to this verse there were at least eight hundred fifty of them, and they ate at the queen's table. They were welcomed into the very court of the king.

> So Ahab sent a message among all the sons of Israel, and brought the prophets together at Mount Carmel.
>
> 1 Kings 18:20

The audience gathered on Mount Carmel to witness the showdown was composed of two groups: the prophets and priests of the false gods, Baal and Asherah, and "the sons of Israel"—that is, the general public, or a representation of the people of the land. The prophets and priests of Baal and Asherah had prompted and promoted the worship of idols, so Elijah addresses them directly throughout most of this epochal event. But many Israelites had willingly followed their wicked, idolatrous leadership, and Elijah wanted to win the people of Israel back to the one true God, even as he also wanted to remove the false prophets and the priests from the land. Thus, knowing that people usually need proof to be convinced, Elijah makes certain that many people will witness this climactic showdown.

> And Elijah came near to all the people and said, "How long will you hesitate between two opinions? If the LORD is God, follow Him; but if Baal, follow him." But the people did not answer him a word.
>
> 1 Kings 18:21

Notice that the people of Israel have already moved into the hard-core camp of idolatry. Yet even there they were divided and indecisive. Some were following Asherah. Some were following Baal. Some were still thinking half-heartedly about the God of heaven. They were undecided.

So Elijah confronts them with the truth: "Listen. How long will you remain lukewarm? How long will you hesitate and vacillate? You can't have it both ways. If the Lord is God, then follow Him. If Baal is God, follow him. Get on one side or the other. It's decision time."

The people didn't say a word. They didn't answer Elijah's challenge. Nor did they argue with him. The easiest thing to do at the hour of decision is to remain uncommitted. Just linger in the neutral zone. And that's what they did. They were silent.

But Elijah wasn't deterred. He stood there all alone, vastly outnumbered but absolutely invincible in God's hands. Arrayed before him were the idol-worshiping, undecided people of the land. Standing by were the eight hundred fifty priests and prophets of Baal and Asherah. No doubt there were idol shrines erected here and there across the summit of Mount Carmel, as there were on most of the mountain peaks of Israel at the time. But Elijah wasn't afraid. He was God's man, and he had a plan they would be unable to ignore or forget. As we say in Texas, "He was fixin' to blow 'em away."

PRESENTATION OF THE PROOF

Elijah's plan was an ingenious one. He was going to provide undeniable proof that the Lord God of heaven was the one true God.

> Then Elijah said to the people, "I alone am left a prophet of the LORD, but Baal's prophets are 450 men.
>
> "Now let them give us two oxen; and let them choose one ox for themselves and cut it up, and place it on the wood, but put no fire under it; and I will prepare the other ox, and lay it on the wood, and I will not put a fire under it.
>
> "Then you call on the name of your god, and I will call on the name of the LORD, and the God who answers by fire, He is God."
>
> 1 Kings 18:22–24a

Elijah's plan was shrewd but fair and simple. Baal was worshiped as the god of the sun (the fire of the universe) and as the all-controlling god of the crops and productivity of the land. Such a god would surely have lightning in his arsenal of weapons! If he could do anything, he ought to be able to start a fire. The same could be said for Jehovah God. Elijah's plan would provide a reasonable test of the power of the rival deities.

And notice the people's response:

And all the people answered and said, "That is a good idea."

1 Kings 18:24b

"Good idea, Elijah. Let's do that," the people responded unanimously.

> So Elijah said to the prophets of Baal, "Choose one ox for yourselves and prepare it first for you are many, and call on the name of your god, but put no fire under it."
> Then they took the ox which was given them and they prepared it and called on the name of Baal from morning until noon saying, "O Baal, answer us." But there was no voice and no one answered. And they leaped about the altar which they made.

1 Kings 18:25–26

They followed Elijah's plan; they carried out his instructions. But when they called upon Baal, nothing happened. From early morning until noon they cried out, "O Baal, answer us." Nothing happened. The heavens were brass. There was no lightening, no fire—not a single stirring in the skies. No one answered. The silence above was deafening.

In desperation the prophets of Baal began leaping around the altar. They were jumping up and down in frenzy, crying out, begging and pleading, trying to attract Baal's attention, trying to make their god bring down fire. It must have been something to behold.

Now if you don't think there is any humor in the Bible, just revisit this scene. Observe what Elijah said.

> And it came about at noon, that Elijah mocked them and said, "Call out with a loud voice, for he is a god; either he is occupied or gone aside, or is on a journey, or perhaps he is asleep and needs to be awakened."

1 Kings 18:27

Can't you just picture it? Elijah is standing over there, leaning against a tree, his arms crossed, watching the prophets of Baal jumping around like a pack of wild animals. After enduring several hours of this nonsense, he says, "Hey, maybe you're not calling loud enough. After all, he's a god! He's probably 'occupied or gone aside.'"

The Hebrew word that is translated *occupied* here suggests that Elijah meant that their God was deep in thought, perhaps preoccupied. "Hey, guys, maybe he's meditating! You gotta yell if you want to get his attention when he's meditating! So . . . yell, guys!"

Or, if he's not meditating, perhaps he has "gone aside." Now that's an interesting expression, and there is some difference of opinion about what it really means. However, some, including my friend and Old Testament scholar, Dr. Ron Allen, believe the wording here suggests that Elijah was taunting them with the idea that Baal may have "stepped into the celestial men's room." Others think the phrase means "he's gone hunting." But whatever the meaning, Elijah's mocking intent is clear.

Then he pushes it even farther. "Maybe your god is on a journey. Or perhaps he has fallen sound asleep. You simply have to yell louder and wake him."

Edersheim, the trustworthy Jewish historian, does a masterful job of painting this particular scene. To do so, he draws on the historical understanding of what often took place in pagan Baal worship.

First rose a comparatively moderate, though already wild, cry to Baal; followed by a dance around the altar, beginning with a swinging motion to and fro. The howl then became louder and louder, and the dance more frantic. They whirled round and round, ran wildly through each other's ranks, always keeping up a circular motion, the head bent low, so that their long disheveled hair swept the ground. Ordinarily the madness now became infectious, and the onlookers joined in the frenzied dance. But Elijah knew how to prevent this. It was noon and for hours they had kept up their wild rites. With cutting taunts and bitter irony Elijah now reminded them that, since Baal was Elohim, the fault must lie with them. He might be otherwise engaged, and they must cry louder. Stung to madness, they became more frantic than before, and what we know as the second and third acts in these feasts ensued. The wild howl passed into piercing demoniacal yells. In their madness the priests bit their arms and cut themselves with two-edged swords which they carried and with lances. As the blood began to flow, the frenzy reached its highest pitch, when first one, then others, commenced to "prophesy," moaned and groaned, then burst into rhapsodic cries, accusing themselves, or speaking to Baal, or uttering incoherent, broken sentences.[1]

What an unforgettable scene of chaos and madness! It was as if the forces of hell had been unleashed and were on display in these out-of-control human bodies. But still, nothing happened in the heavens.

> So they cried with a loud voice and cut themselves according to their custom with swords and lances until the blood gushed out on them.
>
> And it came about when midday was past, that they raved until the time of the offering of the evening sacrifice; but there was no voice, no one answered, and no one paid attention.
>
> 1 Kings 18:28–29

From morning until evening, they called to their god. They even mutilated their own bodies in their frenzy. "But there was no voice." These famous priests and prophets of Baal who, while the masses were suffering under the drought, had been pampered with food and drink at the queen's table, cried out hour after hour, but "no one answered." Picture them in absolute exhaustion, flopping and falling down in the dust, panting, bleeding, and, finally, humiliated. "And no one paid attention."

At that dramatic juncture, Elijah steps onto the scene. This would be his moment of proof—his greatest hour. Everything he had trained for, all he had endured in silence and solitude, now paid off. More importantly, this was *God's* moment of proof.

> Then Elijah said to all the people, "Come near to me." So all the people came near to him. And he repaired the altar of the LORD which had been torn down.

And Elijah took twelve stones according to the number of the tribes of the sons of Jacob, to whom the word of the LORD had come, saying, "Israel shall be your name."

So with the stones he built an altar in the name of the LORD, and he made a trench around the altar, large enough to hold two measures of seed.

Then he arranged the wood and cut the ox in pieces and laid it on the wood. And he said, "Fill four pitchers with water and pour it on the burnt offering and on the wood."

And he said, "Do it a second time," and they did it a second time. And he said, "Do it a third time," and they did it a third time.

And the water flowed around the altar, and he also filled the trench with water.

1 Kings 18:30–35

The first thing Elijah did was rebuild the altar of the Lord, which had been destroyed during this period of idolatry in the land of Israel. He avoided all contact with the altar that had been dedicated to and associated with Baal. If the true fire of heaven from the true God of heaven was to prove to all that Jehovah was the one true God, then an altar built "in the name of the Lord" needed to be constructed to receive that fire. Therefore, using twelve stones representing the twelve tribes of Israel, Elijah built an altar uniquely for the glory of his God.

Notice that Elijah tells the people to fill four pitchers with water. Some commentators believe that the term translated "pitchers" should be "barrels." Either way, the point is that they used several sizeable containers of water to soak the rebuilt altar of God.

Also, some critics of Scripture have a field day with that verse because they say, "If there was such a drought in the land, where would they get this water?" What they fail to take into account is that Mount Carmel is not that far from the Mediterranean Sea, and there was plenty of water there. The people couldn't drink it, of course. But even salt water would do a good job of dampening the wood. So I imagine they trekked down that mountain and got the water, then climbed back up and dumped it on the altar. They made this trip three times, according to Elijah's instructions, until the wood and the offering were soaked and there was enough water left over to fill the trench around the altar. The prophet was determined to prove his point.

> Then it came about at the time of the offering of the evening sacrifice, that Elijah the prophet came near and said, "O LORD, the God of Abraham, Isaac and Israel, today let it be known that Thou art God in Israel, and that I am Thy servant, and that I have done all these things at Thy word.
>
> "Answer me, O LORD, answer me, that this people may know that Thou, O LORD, art God, and that Thou hast turned their heart back again."
>
> 1 Kings 18:36–37

Elijah's prayer was a simple one, but it was a prayer of *faith*. There was no pleading or screaming. No shouting. No frenzied cultic dance. No empty repetition of the same words uttered for hours. Just a plainly spoken request that God would prove to all that He, alone, is Lord.

The contrast is stunning. And the response was immediate: It was a consuming fire . . . and it was convincing.

> Then the fire of the LORD fell, and consumed the burnt offering and the wood and the stones and the dust, and licked up the water that was in the trench.
>
> And when all the people saw it, they fell on their faces; and they said, "The LORD, He is God; the LORD, He is God."
>
> 1 Kings 18:38–39

God answered Elijah's prayer. This not only brought fire, but far more importantly, it turned the hearts of the people back to God. It also rid the land of the prophets of Baal.

> Then Elijah said to them, "Seize the prophets of Baal; do not let one of them escape." So they seized them; and Elijah brought them down to the brook Kishon, and slew them there.
>
> 1 Kings 18:40

Some read that last verse and say, "What an extreme response!" Is it? What would you think of a physician who found a mass of rapidly growing malignant cells in your abdomen and said to you, "I think we'd better remove *some* of those cells"? Or, "I'd like to do just a little *minor* surgery"? No. A good physician would see that deadly mass and would say, "We have to get *all* of those cells out of there, along with any surrounding areas that might be contaminated." That's not extreme. That's essential. That's wise.

The prophets of Baal were an immoral, hostile, and anti-God malignancy in the land of Israel. Elijah knew he had to cut away all evidence of such a godless menace.

TIMELESS TRUTHS FOR MODERN-DAY ELIJAHS

What an unforgettable story, leaving lasting lessons for all. In this great chapter from Elijah's life, I find several ever-relevant principles of truth.

First, *when we are sure that we are in the will of God, we are invincible.*

Nothing makes us more uncertain and insecure than not being sure we are in the will of God. And nothing is more encouraging than knowing for sure that we are. Then, no matter what the circumstances, no matter what happens, we can stand fast.

We can be out of a job but know that we are in the will of God. We can face a threatening situation but know that we are in the will of God. We can have the odds stacked against us but know that we are in the will of God. Nothing intimidates those who know that what they believe is based on what God has said. The equation is never eight hundred fifty against one. It is eight hundred fifty against one plus God.

When we know we're in the will of God, we're invincible.

Never once was Elijah intimidated. In this passage, Elijah spoke eight times, and every time he *commanded.* Yes, every time. He didn't shift, he didn't stutter, he didn't suggest; he leveled a command. He wasn't on the defense; he was on the offense. He knew where he stood. The word to describe that? Invincible.

Second, *divided allegiance is as wrong as open idolatry.*

"How long will you hesitate between two opinions?" Elijah asks the people of Israel. The easiest thing to do when you are outnumbered or overwhelmed is to remain in that mediocre state of noncommitment. That was where the people of Israel lived, but Elijah never dwelt there. He told them, "You cannot continue in this period of divided allegiance any longer."

The strongest words that were given to the seven churches mentioned in the Book of Revelation, chapters 2 and 3, were given to the church at Laodicea. And the reason is clear: They were uncommitted. They were neither hot nor cold. "'I know your deeds, that you are neither cold nor hot; I would that you were cold or hot. So because you are lukewarm, and neither hot nor cold, I will spit you out of My mouth'" (Rev. 3:15-16).

Get off the fence of indecision, Elijah told the people of Israel. Either you are *for* God or *against* Him.

Perhaps you have known God for many years but have never truly been committed to Him. Now is the time to change that. Stop hiding your love for and commitment to Christ. Let the word out! Tactfully yet fearlessly speak devotedly of your faith. Start now. There are so many strategic ways God can use you in your business, your profession, your school, your neighborhood. You don't agree with the ungodly cultural drift that's happening around you? Say so! You sense an erosion of spirituality at your church . . . and you're serving in a leadership capacity? Address it! Neutrality in the hour of decision is a curse leading to tragic consequences.

Third, *our most effective tool is the prayer of faith.*

When it came down to the wire, when Baal had failed and God was about to do His work, the one instrument that Elijah employed was prayer.

Isn't it amazing how often people try everything but that? It's like the old saying: "When everything else fails, read the instructions." So it goes with prayer. When everything else fails, try prayer. "Okay, okay . . . maybe we should pray about it." But Elijah didn't use prayer as a last resort. Prayer was his first and only resort. A simple prayer of faith was his major contact with the living Lord. It set everything in motion.

Let me ask you a straight-out question: Do you, personally, pray? Now notice that I didn't say, "Do you listen when the preacher prays or when your parents pray?" I didn't say, "Do you know a good Bible study on prayer?" I didn't even say, "Have you taught on prayer?" I asked: "Do *you,* personally, pray?" Can you look back over the last seven days and pinpoint times you deliberately set aside for prayer? Even just a solid ten or fifteen minutes of uninterrupted time with God?

Howard Taylor once wrote of his father's discipline in prayer: "The sun never rose on China for forty years but that God did not find my father [Hudson Taylor] in prayer."

The most effective tool of the believer is prayer.

Fourth, *never underestimate the power of one totally dedicated life.*

This entire incident revolves around one dedicated life—the life of Elijah. He was a man all alone, overwhelmingly outnumbered by a hostile king, the king's wicked and powerful wife, eight hundred fifty pagan prophets and priests of Baal, and countless numbers of unbelieving Israelites. Yet all of them were silenced and intimidated by this one dedicated man of God.

I think back to the dedicated people who have influenced my own life. Through the years, I have come in contact with thousands of people: during my formative years at home, in high school, in the Marine Corps, in churches, in seminary, in ministry. Missionaries. Statesmen and stateswomen. Scholars. Educators. Athletes. Coaches. Professionals. Friends. Neighbors. But I must tell you, only a handful of men and women have truly influenced my life, and invariably it was because of their dedication and commitment. Think about that in your own life: Who are the people who have influenced you and why? Stop long enough to name them. Then turn the question back on yourself. Ask yourself this searching question: How many people have I influenced by my life? That's a question we can't really answer, of course, but it is a question that should challenge how we live.

How exciting it would be if, through your own dedication to Jesus Christ, you could influence one person this next week, either by leading him to Jesus or by building her up in the faith. Sound impossible? You know it's not. The Bible and the history of the church are filled with stories of the difference one person's dedication to God has made.

Elijah staged a magnificent showdown with the prophets of Baal. But the greatest showdown of all time was at Calvary, where the enemy of God was defeated by the sacrifice of God's own Son. Why? Because God had one dedicated life He could count on: His own dear Son, Jesus. In fact, the difference He made changed all of history.

That brings me to an interesting point and answers the question I posed at the beginning of this chapter: If *Time, Newsweek,* and *People* magazines had been around at the turn of the century in 700 B.C., would they have included Elijah on one of their lists? Remember all those lists I mentioned? Well, of all the lists of "significant people" I saw at the turn of the millennium, not one—not even those that went back to ancient days—mentioned the name of Jesus Christ, which proves that those who make the greatest spiritual difference, those who have the strongest godly influence on others, will not be remembered by the media . . . but they'll certainly be rewarded by God.

Can you imagine the reward awaiting Elijah?

Now Elijah said to Ahab, "Go up, eat and drink; for there is the sound of the roar of a heavy shower." So Ahab went up to eat and drink. But Elijah went up to the top of Carmel; and he crouched down on the earth, and put his face between his knees. And he said to his servant, "Go up now, look toward the sea." So he went up and looked and said, "There is nothing." And he said, "Go back" seven times. And it came about at the seventh time, that he said, "Behold, a cloud as small as a man's hand is coming up from the sea." And he said, "Go up, say to Ahab, 'Prepare your chariot and go down, so that the heavy shower does not stop you.'" So it came about in a little while, that the sky grew black with clouds and wind, and there was a heavy shower. And Ahab rode and went to Jezreel. Then the hand of the LORD was on Elijah, and he girded up his loins and outran Ahab to Jezreel.

1 KINGS 18:41–46

CHAPTER SIX

A Man of God . . . A Promise of God

G od keeps His promises. It's a major part of His immutable nature. He doesn't hold out hope with nice-sounding words, then renege on what He said He would do. God is neither fickle nor moody. And He never lies. As my own father used to say of people with integrity, "His word is His bond."

When you stop to think about it, it was because of a promise of God that Elijah came on the biblical scene in the first place. It was the prophet's unpopular task to announce God's message to the king. That message had to do with a terrible drought that was coming: The drought would last for years, and it would not end "except by my word"(1 Kings 17:1). That message was not only a wake-up call to get Ahab's attention, it was also a not-so-subtle reminder that, even though Ahab thought he was in charge, "the God of Israel lives" and He, alone, determines what will happen when.

Elijah's heroism in standing before the king of the land and telling him what he didn't want to hear came from the man of God's confidence in the word of his Lord. The Master of heaven had spoken, and that was the message Elijah brought to the attention of Ahab. God promised a drought, and nothing Ahab could do would keep it from arriving or diminish its devastating results. Furthermore, God had assured the prophet, who passed it on to the king, that the drought would not end until God determined it would end. Period. End of announcement. Exit Elijah. Bring on the drought.

The very thing that God had communicated through His prophet came to pass. Exactly as God promised, there was not a drop of rain to relieve the scorched earth. The land became parched and barren as months passed, turning into years. Rivers no longer flowed, streams dried up, wells ran dry, crops burned to a brown crisp, animals died, and the king found him-self totally helpless to interfere with God's act of judgment.

God keeps His promises. Agree with it or not, His word is final.

As we have seen, many things were happening behind the scenes dur-ing this drought. God's servant was put through the paces as his Lord prepared him for the mission He had in mind for him. The only "headline news" was the dreadful drought, day after monotonous day. But behind the scenes, unheralded, God was working His sovereign will in the heart of His man, Elijah, just as faithfully as He was sustaining the drought across the land of Israel. And even though it may have seemed that He had for-gotten all about His earlier statement regarding the land, He never forgets anything He promises. That's right . . . never.

God's agenda continues to unfold right on schedule, even when there is not a shred of evidence that He remembers. Even when the most extreme events transpire and "life just doesn't seem fair," God is there, carrying out His providential plan exactly as He pre-arranged it. And to complicate matters, He doesn't feel the need to clear any part of that plan with any earthling. Why should He? Chances are good we'd not agree anyway. And so we wait. And wait. And wait. Our faith is stretched because, I repeat, there is absolutely nothing that makes us think He even remembers the promise He made.

And then suddenly, without warning, He keeps His word. He decides it's time to step back into time as we reckon it (which is not at all the realm in which He exists) to make good on His promise. It's the right moment. Enough waiting. And wouldn't you know it? As He said He would, He acts. Changes occur just as He promised. It's happened like that ever since our Creator has been dealing with His creatures. Yet we still doubt. We still worry. We still wonder if He will remember. Strangely, we just don't get it.

Now, back to our friend Elijah. In the first verse in 1 Kings 18 there is an eloquent phrase: "The word of the Lord came to Elijah in the third year." Three years! That's an incredibly long time to go without rain. We can't even imagine it, can we? But God was up to something. By now, not even those false prophets could garner much credibility. All repetitious prayers and rituals and voodoo tactics had proven useless. Is it any wonder that Elijah had the people's attention when he challenged the prophets of Baal and Asherah to a public showdown with Jehovah God? By now, they were willing to try anything. Elijah didn't have to plead for their cooperation.

And is it any wonder that, when God proved Himself to them, the people "fell on their faces" and immediately acknowledged, "The Lord, He is God; the Lord, He is God" (18:39)? And when Elijah told those same people to seize the prophets and not let one of them escape, he didn't have to beg them; the people of Israel had had enough of those idolatrous fools! The fire from heaven may have convinced them, but the never-ending drought had already sucked dry most of the confidence they'd had in the pagan leaders they had once followed. God's delay worked wonders when the choice between who was worthy of worship needed to be made. Natural calamities normally turn hearts *toward* God, not *from* Him.

But look again at that first verse in 1 Kings 18, and you will find another promise of God. Elijah was more than ready to hear this one! "I will send rain on the face of the earth," God said.

Finally. What relief that promise must have brought. I find it interesting that God's prophet had never once complained about the drought, even though the very brook from which his water supply came had dried up, and even though it must have been as dreadfully difficult for him as it was for the others in the land of Israel. But the difference between Elijah and the others was simple: He knew God would one day fulfill His promise and bring rain. Until then, Elijah would wait, never doubting, because he was fully persuaded of something most of us, at one time or another, doubt: God keeps His promises.

SOME CLARIFYING COMMENTS ABOUT PROMISES

The Bible is full of promises—thousands of them. In fact, I recall reading many years ago in a national periodical that someone had taken the time to count all the promises in the Bible and had come up with almost seven thousand five hundred of them! I have not counted all of them, therefore I'm not able to verify that figure, but it is safe to say there are indeed several thousand promises in the Word of God. Admittedly, they are not all as specific and direct as the ones we've reviewed from Elijah's day, but there are numerous promises punctuated throughout the Scriptures.

The question worth pondering is one I've seldom heard addressed: Can we claim every one of those promises personally? I can still remember singing a little chorus in Sunday school: "Every promise in the Book is mine. . . ." But that isn't true. That's a major overstatement. As a matter of fact, one of the best ways to get yourself in trouble really fast is to start claiming every biblical promise you come across. Though some would encourage us to go in that direction, I need to warn you: That's a dangerous practice.

In an excellent book that speaks to this very issue, *Protestant Biblical Interpretation*, I find some extremely helpful counsel. The author, theologian Bernard Ramm, warns against trying to force any and every Bible promise into our specific situations. As a case in point, he cites the example of a man who, during World War II, wondered if he should enlist in the military service, or join the Merchant Marines, or seek a theological waiver. Like many Christians, he turned to his Bible for help and, while reading in the Psalms, he found a reference to "those who go down to the sea in ships" (Psalm 107:23). He took that personally and literally, claiming it as a direct order from God to enlist in the United States Navy.

> The action could not be based upon any sensible exegetical principle, nor upon any spiritual principle. It was a haphazard coincidence between the verse that had the word *seas* in it and the United States Navy.[1]

Unfortunately, that young man is not alone in employing this method of determining God's message to them. He meant well, but he made the common mistake that so many untaught Christians make. Ignoring the context and overlooking the possibility that certain promises were given to one specific person for one particular situation, these individuals claim that all the biblical promises are there for us today, in whatever circumstance we may find ourselves. Those who do this will someday find themselves woefully confused, however, for not all promises found in the Bible are for us to claim. Nor were they ever meant to be.

Don't misunderstand. The Bible is, indeed, God's inerrant Word. And His Word is authoritative, profitable, and reliable. God has preserved it for us to guide us into His will, to assist us in our struggles, to comfort us in our sorrows, and to equip us to stand firm through trials. There is no question about any of that. But this is not to say that every single promise that has been recorded in the pages of Holy Scripture is written for us to claim and count on.

So please stay with me through this important section of clarification. We're not going to lose sight of Elijah, but we do need to understand certain things about God's promises.

PERSONAL OR UNIVERSAL?

Before you and I can claim any promise, we need to determine in which category it falls. Is it one of those promises that was meant for a unique situation and given to a specific person or group of individuals who lived in the days in which Scripture was being written? Such personal and direct promises applied to them and only them, at that time, for specific purposes God reserved for their time and place. Or is the promise one of the many general promises that have a much broader-based universal appeal and application?

Is it one of those unique promises, not addressed to us, but specifically meant for another? Was that the setting in which God had that promise recorded? Or did He intend it for anyone in any generation?

To determine the answer, we must check the context, read the passage carefully, and employ great discernment. If it's the former, then stay away from it. Don't go there. Refuse to set your heart on that promise as though it's for you. Otherwise, you're in for a massive disappointment and future disillusionment! However, if it is in the latter category, claim it. Count on it. Believe it. I would even say, more often than not, *memorize* it! It could prove to be a source of enormous comfort and reassurance in the days ahead.

An example of a promise to a specific individual in a unique situation would be God's promise to Joshua in Joshua 6:

> And you shall march around the city, all the men of war circling the city once. You shall do so for six days. Also seven priests shall carry seven trumpets of rams' horns before the ark; then on the seventh day you shall march around the city seven times, and the priests shall blow the trumpets.
>
> And it shall be that when they make a long blast with the ram's horn, and when you hear the sound of the trumpet, all the people shall shout with a great shout; and the wall of the city will fall down flat, and the people will go up every man straight ahead.
>
> Joshua 6:3–5

That promise was given to Joshua for his specific situation at the city of Jericho. It is not a promise to be claimed by any other military commander, past or present, in attempting to take a city.

Or consider the promise in Mark 16:18: "They will pick up serpents, and if they drink any deadly poison, it shall not hurt them."

Certain groups of people today use this verse as a basis for their beliefs, claiming this as a personal promise for their disciples. Consider this newspaper report headlined, "2 Holiness Preachers Die in a Test of Faith."

> Two Holiness preachers who had survived the bites of poisonous snakes tested their faith with strychnine and died a few hours after drinking the poison. . . . Cocke County officers [of Tennessee] said copperheads and rattlesnakes were handled at the . . . religious service Saturday night. After the snakes had been handled, Mr. Williams and Mr. Pack drank strychnine as a further test of their faith [based on] Mark 16:18.[2]

I repeat the warning: It is dangerous to claim a promise out of its context, apart from its primary setting and away from its original meaning. If it is a personal promise in a unique situation, stay away from it. That promise is not for you and me.

If, however, the promise is a universal one, then claim it joyfully. Several in this category come to mind:

> For as high as the heavens are above the earth,
> So great is His lovingkindness toward those who fear Him.
> As far as the east is from the west,
> So far has He removed our transgressions from us.
> Just as a father has compassion on his children,
> So the LORD has compassion on those who fear Him.
>
> Psalm 103:11–13

> Trust in the LORD with all your heart,
> And do not lean on your own understanding.
> In all your ways acknowledge Him,
> And He will make your paths straight.
>
> Proverbs 3:5–6

> Do not fear, for I am with you;
> Do not anxiously look about you, for I am your God.
> I will strengthen you, surely I will help you,
> Surely I will uphold you with My righteous right hand.
>
> Isaiah 41:10

> Ask, and it shall be given to you; seek, and you shall find; knock, and it shall be opened to you.
>
> For everyone who asks receives, and he who seeks finds, and to him who knocks it shall be opened.
>
> Matthew 7:7–8

For the Scripture says, "Whoever believes in Him will not be disappointed." For there is no distinction between Jew and Greek; for the same Lord is Lord of all, abounding in riches for all who call upon Him; for "Whoever will call upon the name of the Lord will be saved."

Romans 10:11–13

And my God shall supply all your needs according to His riches in glory in Christ Jesus.

Philippians 4:19

For the Lord Himself will descend from heaven with a shout, with the voice of the archangel, and with the trumpet of God; and the dead in Christ shall rise first. Then we who are alive and remain shall be caught up together with them in the clouds to meet the Lord in the air, and thus we shall always be with the Lord.

1 Thessalonians 4:16–17

Beloved, do not be surprised at the fiery ordeal among you, which comes upon you for your testing, as though some strange thing were happening to you; but to the degree that you share the sufferings of Christ, keep on rejoicing; so that also at the revelation of His glory, you may rejoice with exultation. If you are reviled for the name of Christ, you are blessed, because the Spirit of glory and of God rests upon you. By no means let any of you suffer as a murderer, or thief, or evildoer, or a troublesome meddler; but if anyone suffers as a Christian, let him not feel ashamed, but in that name let him glorify God. For it is time for judgment to begin with the household of God; and if it begins with us first, what will be the outcome for those who do not obey the gospel of God?

1 Peter 4:12–17

CONDITIONAL OR UNCONDITIONAL?

Even with those promises we may claim, however, we need further discernment. We must determine whether they are conditional or unconditional.

A conditional promise will not be fulfilled until *we* have kept our part: the condition on which the promise hangs. For example, consider 1 John 1:9: "If we confess our sins, He is faithful and righteous to forgive us our sins and to cleanse us from all unrighteousness." If I refuse to confess my sins, I cannot expect my holy, heavenly Father immediately and automatically to forgive my carnality. In other words, I cannot claim the promise of God's forgiveness until I've done my part (the condition), which is to confess my sins.

Matthew 21:22 says, "'And all things you ask in prayer, believing, you shall receive.'" People point to that verse and say, "There is my promise. I can ask God for such and such and I will receive it." But they often overlook the condition in Scripture that says, "If I regard wickedness in my heart, the Lord will not hear" (Psalm 66:18). In other words, a sinful, disobedient heart, though it may be the heart of a child of God, does not arouse the activity of God. The vessel must be clean. That's the condition that must be met.

Unconditional promises are just that: *unconditional.* They are neither qualified nor limited. What is promised by God will occur, regardless of anyone's response. Several come to mind.

Thy word is a lamp to my feet, And a light to my path.

Psalm 119:105

And all the inhabitants of the earth are accounted as nothing. But He does according to His will in the host of Heaven and among the inhabitants of earth: And no one can ward off His hand or say to Him, "What hast Thou done?"

Daniel 4:35

And my God shall supply all your needs according to His riches in glory in Christ Jesus.

Philippians 4:19

For the grace of God has appeared, bringing salvation to all men.

Titus 2:11

For God is not unjust so as to forget your work and the love which you have shown toward His name, in having ministered and in still ministering to the saints.

Hebrews 6:10

The Bible is God's inspired truth. It is wholly trustworthy, for God is trustworthy. It is our sacred guide, written for our instruction. But it is not some kind of rabbit's foot we carry about, hoping for good luck. It is to be read intelligently, interpreted carefully, treated respectfully, handled wisely, and applied correctly. Down through the centuries the Scriptures have been misread and twisted, forced and abused, by saints and sinners alike. Often, those who go farthest away from God's intended direction are those who pull promises from their original and unique settings and push them, inappropriately, into applications they were never meant to fulfill.

ELIJAH CLAIMS A PROMISE

For three long years and more the land of Israel had been without rain or dew. God had told Elijah to tell King Ahab that because of his sinfulness, a terrible drought would come upon the land. And that is exactly what happened. The land became parched and cracked and broken. The results, as we have seen, were death and desolation.

Then, in His own time, God came to the rescue of Israel. He broke the silence and instructed His servant to declare His will.

> Now it came about after many days, that the word of the LORD came
> to Elijah in the third year, saying, "Go, show yourself to Ahab, and I
> will send rain on the face of the earth."
>
> 1 Kings 18:1

When God speaks to His prophet, He offers him a promise. Now, in light
of what we have learned about promises, let's analyze this one.

First, it is a personal promise made to one individual (Elijah) in a specific situation. Second, it is a conditional promise. "Elijah, you go show
yourself to Ahab" (that's the condition—that's Elijah's part), says God, "and
I will send rain" (that's the promise—that's God's part). God was not going
to send rain until and unless Elijah went to Ahab.

In the last chapter, we saw that Elijah met that condition. He went to
Ahab. Then he climbed to the top of Mount Carmel and prayed fire down
from heaven, by the marvelous power of God. The result was dramatic:
The prophets of Baal were slaughtered, and God proved that He, alone,
was the Lord of heaven and earth. But Elijah wasn't through yet. The land
was still parched by drought, and God had promised to send rain. Elijah
hadn't forgotten that promise. And knowing that God keeps His promises,
Elijah had no problem issuing a command to the king of the land.

> Now Elijah said to Ahab, "Go up, eat and drink; for there is the sound
> of the roar of a heavy shower."
>
> 1 Kings 18:41

Now when we read that, we get the impression that Elijah actually heard the
rain pouring down, or at least the thunderous rumblings of an approaching
storm. "You can celebrate now, Ahab. The drought is over," he said.

But when I examine this verse in the context of the following verses, I
am convinced that up to this point there was not a cloud in the sky—not
a flash of lightning or a roll of thunder. So what was the sound? Well, I
believe that Elijah was hearing the sound of God's voice and the promise
He had made—that if Elijah went to Ahab, then He (God) would send

rain. In fact, the Hebrew word that is translated "sound" here is translated "voice," or refers to the sound of a voice, in other places in Scripture.

Elijah was certain that the rain was coming, not because he heard the sound of rain itself nor even far-off thunder, but because he was claiming the stated promise of God. And he claimed that promise through prayer.

KNEELING ON THE PROMISE

So Ahab went up to eat and drink. But Elijah went up to the top of Carmel; and he crouched down on the earth, and put his face between his knees.

And he said to his servant, "Go up now, look toward the sea." So he went up and looked and said, "There is nothing." And he said, "Go back" seven times.

And it came about at the seventh time, that he said, "Behold, a cloud as small as a man's hand is coming up from the sea." And he said, "Go up, say to Ahab, 'Prepare your chariot and go down, so that the heavy shower does not stop you.'"

1 Kings 18:42–44

When we look closely, we find five wonderful components in Elijah's prayer as he claimed God's promise.

First, *he separated himself.* "Elijah went up to the top of Carmel."

Never underestimate the place of prayer. I've mentioned this before, but it's worth repeating. I'm convinced that one of the reasons we are so lax in prayer is that we have never prepared a place to meet with God. When you want to draw near to the heart of God, you have to get away from the din, away from the confusion, away from the noise and distractions. Now granted, you can't always climb or drive up to a mountaintop. You can't always get to the sea. But you do need a place apart—a place where you can separate yourself from the distractions of daily life and meet, alone, with God.

Our great forefather Abraham frequently returned to Bethel, the place where he had first built an altar and called upon the name of the Lord. It was there, in that familiar, intimate setting, that he found refreshing fellowship with his Lord. It was there that he received cleansing from his failures. Abraham separated himself and got alone with God.

We, too, need such a place. It can be a place as simple as a closet or a room where you can shut the door and be alone. That's all you need—just a place to be alone with God to pray, to wait, to seek His will, to claim His promises.

Second, *Elijah humbled himself.* "He crouched down on the earth, and put his face between his knees."

The most vulnerable moment is right after a great victory. Humility does not follow readily on the heels of awards and achievement. Yet Elijah, who had just come through the greatest and certainly the most public victory of his life, was not arrogant. He went right back to Mount Carmel—back to the very site of that triumph—and humbled himself before God.

The best attitude in prayer is an attitude of humility. Elijah offers us an outstanding model and example.

When seeking a title for this book, I naturally was drawn to Elijah's courage and fortitude. "Heroism" seemed a synonym for his name. When we think of Elijah, we think of a man of invincible power, one who wasn't afraid to face down the greatest powers of his day—pagan priests and a wicked monarch and his evil consort. Yet the more I studied his life, probing to find the source of his courage, the more I kept coming back to moments like this one, when he humbled himself before the greatest power of all. Regardless of his impressive achievements, Elijah never forgot the importance of the principle that the apostle Peter mentioned centuries later:

> Humble yourselves, therefore, under the mighty hand of God, that
> He may exalt you at the proper time.
>
> 1 Peter 5:6

Heroism, yes. Elijah definitely exhibited that quality. But humility throughout his life and ministry—that was at the core of Elijah's character.

Third, *Elijah was specific.* "Go up now," he told his servant, "and look toward the sea."

Elijah told his servant to look for one thing: a sign of rain. God had promised rain, and that was what Elijah was expecting, confident God would keep that precise promise.

Be specific in your prayer life. If you need a job, pray for a job. If you're an engineer, ask God to open up an engineering position for you, or something related for which you are qualified. If you're in sales, ask God for a sales position. If you need fifteen hundred dollars for tuition, ask for that amount. If some fear has you in its grasp, name that fear and ask specifically for relief from it. If it is envy you're struggling with, call it by name. "We need," as one of my mentors used to say, "to guard against the slimy ooze of indefiniteness." Learn from Elijah's example. Make your petitions specific.

Fourth, *Elijah was persistent.* "And he said, 'Go back' seven times."

When testing comes, it often comes when we have to wait. We want the answer fast—right now. It's difficult to wait. Waiting, however, brings needed perspective. And we learn, as well, to be patient. God's timing is not based on our clock. He is never late, but He often deliberately "delays." He loves it when we "go back seven times." Or seventeen. Or seventy! There are some things for which I have prayed consistently, on and off, for six and a half years. One thing, specifically, for over eight years.

Elijah knew that the answer to his prayer would come in God's own time, and it would come only because God had promised that it would. Remember our theme in this chapter? *God keeps His promises.* Because he knew this . . . believed this . . . Elijah would wait. As he did, he persisted in humbling himself before God. Fervency and faith go hand in hand.

Fifth, *Elijah was expectant.* "And it came about at the seventh time, that he said, 'Behold, a cloud as small as a man's hand is coming up from the sea.'"

All that Elijah had to go on was a tiny cloud, no bigger than a man's hand, in the midst of that vast expanse of sea and sky. But that was enough! He had such faith in God's promise that he acted upon what he expected to happen.

> And he said, "Go up, say to Ahab, 'Prepare your chariot and go down, so that the heavy shower does not stop you.'"
>
> 1 Kings 18:44b

All Elijah saw was a tiny cloud, but he said, in effect, "Ahab, put the rain tires on your chariot. The deluge is coming!" The human eye saw only a little cloud, but the eye of faith saw the promise of God. Ahab would have shrugged, "So, what's the big deal?" But Elijah shouted within himself, *"Finally, God is keeping His word!"*

Do you live expectantly? Do the little things excite you? Do you imagine the improbable and expect the impossible? Life is full and running over with opportunities to see God's hand in little things. Only the most sensitive of His servants see them, smile, and live on tiptoe.

Children can teach us a lot about this kind of expectancy. Did you ever listen to a child pray? Their faith knows no bounds. And who are the least surprised people when God answers prayer? The children.

But then we get older and we grow too sophisticated for that. We use phrases like, "Let's be realistic about this." We lose that expectancy, that urgency of hope, that delightful, childlike, wide-eyed joy of faith that keeps us full of anticipation and excitement. May God deliver us from a grim, stoic, stale shrug of the shoulders! "Look, I haven't changed," He says. "I still delight in doing impossible things. I love to surprise you!"

Elijah's God was the God who kept His promises. He was the God of impossible things. So Elijah said to Ahab, "Get ready. The rain's coming. I know, because there's a tiny little cloud out there that's getting ready to unload God's abundance."

> So it came about in a little while, that the sky grew black with clouds and wind, and there was a heavy shower. And Ahab rose and went to Jezreel.
>
> Then the hand of the LORD was on Elijah, and he girded up his loins and outran Ahab to Jezreel.
>
> 1 Kings 18:45–46

I love this scene! Every time I read it, I almost laugh out loud.

Ahab is racing in his chariot across the land, trying to outrun the storm. He hasn't seen rain for so long that he doesn't know whether to spit or wind his watch! And then along comes Elijah, running like mad behind him, gaining on him, passing him, outrunning him all the way to Jezreel—about thirteen miles away—on foot!

If you ever have the opportunity to travel to the Holy Land, do so. Take it from me, you will never regret it. Every time I'm there, another section of the Scriptures jumps off the page. Here's an example.

The last time I was in Israel, as always, our group went up to Mount Carmel. (If you will remember, that's the place I mentioned in the previous chapter where the imposing statue of Elijah stands.) There is an old church on the mountain, and when you climb to the top of the building, you encounter a breathtaking view. Stretching out before you is the vast, sweeping Valley of Jezreel. What an eye-opening sight! You can see for miles.

With a little sanctified imagination, you can see that hand-sized cloud starting to form in the distance, you can watch the sky grow dark, and you can hear the big drops of rain start to splash . . . and look! There's the old prophet, Elijah, running, running, running, faster and faster, hitching his robe up around his thighs as he catches up with Ahab's chariot, which is starting to get bogged down in the mud churned up by the torrential downpour. It's a *wonderful* sight!

And then, while you're standing there smiling, thinking you're all alone with Elijah and Ahab . . . and God . . . some other tour group behind you wonders what you're laughing at and why you don't move out of their way so they can see what's so amusing. Some travelers just don't get it.

Can you imagine the thoughts that must have been running through King Ahab's mind about this prophet of God, who was sprinting alongside his chariot in the rain? At the very least he must have thought the man bizarre. Strange. Weird.

But Elijah wasn't weird. "The hand of the Lord was on him," and he lived expectantly. And if that's weird, well, then, I want to be weird. It's not easy to be in Elijah's league. It's not easy, but it's also not impossible. I'd like to start a brand-new club that only Elijah-types can join. What fun we could have outrunning chariots, shocking the Ahabs that are bogged down in the mud of monotony and mediocrity, held back from the fun of running with God through the downpour of His blessings!

Here's what James says:

The effective prayer of a righteous man can accomplish much.

Elijah was a man with a nature like ours, and he prayed earnestly that it might not rain; and it did not rain on the earth for three years and six months.

And he prayed again, and the sky poured rain, and the earth produced its fruit.

James 5:16b–18

We read about Elijah and we say, "Wow, he's in the big leagues. He's a spiritual giant. I'm a pygmy in comparison to him. He's in another world entirely." Not true. Look again.

James doesn't say, "Elijah was a mighty prophet of God." He doesn't say, "Elijah was a powerful worker of miracles." He doesn't say, "Elijah was a model no man can match."

James says, "Elijah was a man with a nature like ours."

That means he was flesh and blood, muscle and bone. As we're about to see, he got really discouraged, and he had some huge disappointments. He had faults and failures and doubts. He was just a man, with a nature like yours and mine. He may have been a man of heroism and humility, but never forget his humanity. Elijah was our kind of man!

So, what kind of man was Elijah?

Well, he wasn't afraid to square off with the king of the land or take on the prophets of Baal. The guy had guts, no question. But he wasn't too powerful to pray . . . or too confident to wait . . . or too sophisticated to see rain in the tiny cloud . . . or too proud to pull up his robe and run like a spotted ape down the mountain in the rain and mud, like the roadrunner, thinking, *"C'mon, Ahab . . . catch me if you can!"*

No wonder Elijah is the kind of man we admire. Isn't it exciting to know we serve the same God he served? Isn't it thrilling to think we can trust the same God he trusted?

And what kind of God is that? He's the God who makes promises and keeps them.

Now Ahab told Jezebel all that Elijah had done, and how he had killed all the prophets with the sword. Then Jezebel sent a messenger to Elijah, saying, "So may the gods do to me and even more, if I do not make your life as the life of one of them by tomorrow about this time." And he was afraid and arose and ran for his life and came to Beersheba, which belongs to Judah, and left his servant there. But he himself went a day's journey into the wilderness, and came and sat down under a juniper tree; and he requested for himself that he might die, and said, "It is enough; now, O LORD, take my life, for I am not better than my fathers." And he lay down and slept under a juniper tree; and behold, there was an angel touching him, and he said to him, "Arise, eat." Then he looked and behold, there was at his head a bread cake baked on hot stones, and a jar of water. So he ate and drank and lay down again. And the angel of the LORD came again a second time and touched him and said, "Arise, eat, because the journey is too great for you." So he arose and ate and drank, and went in the strength of that food forty days and forty nights to Horeb, the mountain of God. Then he came there to a cave, and lodged there; and behold, the word of the LORD came to him, and He said to him, "What are you doing here, Elijah?" And he said, "I have been very zealous for the LORD, the God of hosts; for the sons of Israel have forsaken Thy covenant, torn down Thine altars and killed Thy prophets with the sword. And I alone am left; and they seek my life, to take it away." So He said, "Go forth, and stand on the mountain before the LORD." And behold, the LORD was passing by! And a great and strong wind was rending the mountains and breaking in pieces the rocks before the LORD; but the LORD was not in the wind. And after the wind an earthquake, but the LORD was not in the earthquake. And after the earthquake, a fire, but the LORD was not in the fire; and after the fire a sound of a gentle blowing. And it came about when Elijah heard it, that he wrapped his face in his mantle, and went out and stood in the entrance of the cave. And behold, a voice came to him and said, "What are you doing here, Elijah?" Then he said, "I have been very zealous for the LORD, the God of hosts; for the sons of Israel have forsaken They covenant, torn down Thine altars and killed Thy prophets with the sword. And I alone am left; and they seek my life, to take it away." And the LORD said to him, "Go, return on your way to the wilderness of Damascus, and when you have arrived, you shall anoint Hazael king over Aram; and Jehu the son of Nimshi you shall anoint king over Israel; and Elisha the son of Shaphat of Abel-meholah you shall anoint as prophet in your place. And it shall come about, the one who escapes from the sword of Hazael, Jehu shall put to death, and the one who escapes from the sword of Jehu, Elisha shall put to death. Yet I will leave 7,000 in Israel, all the knees that have not bowed to Baal and every mouth that has not kissed him." So he departed from there and found Elisha the son of Shaphat, while he was plowing with twelve pairs of oxen before him, and he with the twelfth. And Elijah passed over to him and threw his mantle on him. And he left the oxen and ran after Elijah and said, "Please let me kiss my father and my mother, then I will follow you." And he said to him, "Go back again, for what have I done to you?" So he returned from following him, and took the pair of oxen and sacrificed them and boiled their flesh with the implements of the oxen, and gave it to the people and they ate. Then he arose and followed Elijah and minis-tered to him.

1 KINGS 19:1–21

Chapter Seven

Sure Cure for the Blues

Elijah was an heroic prophet, without question. He was also a man of great humility, as we have seen. But let's not forget that he was just a man—a human being, subject to the human condition, as we all are. He suffered discouragement, despondency, and depression. On one occasion, he couldn't shake it.

If you are a student of Scripture, you know that such feelings were not uncommon among many of those we would consider successful men of God. Moses once became so blue and discouraged that he asked God to take his life. Jonah, after the great revival at Nineveh, did the very same thing. Paul "despaired even of life" at a certain point in his Asian ministry (2 Corinthians 1:8). So, it is not surprising that at this point in Elijah's life the great prophet hit bottom. For several years he had stood strong amidst and against almost insurmountable odds and circumstances. But now, after a great victory, he dropped into the throes of discouragement and total despair.

I'm glad that this chapter has been included in Scripture. I'm glad that when God paints the portraits of His men and women, He paints them warts and all. He doesn't ignore their weaknesses or hide their frailties.

THE CAST OF MAJOR PLAYERS

We find four personalities involved in this sad segment of Elijah's life: Ahab, Jezebel, Elijah, and God.

First, we have Ahab, the king, who was dominated by his wife, Jezebel.

> Now Ahab told Jezebel all that Elijah had done, and how he had killed all the prophets with the sword.
>
> 1 Kings 19:1

Ahab fell apart under pressure. When that happened, he relied on his wife to get him through and to give him the strength that he needed to survive. Ahab's insecurity would have been unhealthy enough if Jezebel had been a good woman, but she was anything but that. Ahab also leaned on his wife to carry out his responsibilities as a monarch. Theirs was more a needy child/mother relationship than a mature husband/wife relationship.

And when Ahab turned to Jezebel, she loved it. In fact, she took over.

> Then Jezebel sent a messenger to Elijah, saying, "So may the gods do to me and even more, if I do not make your life as the life of one of them by tomorrow about this time."
>
> 1 Kings 19:2

Jezebel fits to a T the image of a domineering wife. First, she quickly took matters into her own hands. Second, she did her husband's job her own way. Third, she turned to intimidation and schemes when she saw her weak-willed husband crumbling under pressure.

We see the latter in the threatening message Jezebel sent to Elijah: "So may the gods do to me and even more, if I do not make your life as the life of one of them by tomorrow about this time." That's classic intimidation. In effect, Jezebel was saying to Elijah, "By this time tomorrow I'm going to have you killed."

But look at the one she is threatening. This is Elijah, man of heroism—the prophet of God who has been to Cherith, the man of God who has been to Zarephath, the hero of faith who has faced down the prophets of Baal and called down fire from heaven. This is Elijah, man of humility, who trusted when God gave a promise, who prayed when he needed God to give strength. Surely, this man would never fall for that wicked woman's scheme of intimidation. Or would he? Well, in this case, he did.

He's a man, he's human, just like us, remember. Since this is true, we shouldn't be shocked to read that . . .

> he was afraid and arose and ran for his life and came to Beersheba, which belongs to Judah, and left his servant there.
>
> But he himself went a day's journey into the wilderness, and came and sat down under a juniper tree; and he requested for himself that he might die, and said, "It is enough; now, O Lord, take my life, for I am not better than my fathers."
>
> 1 Kings 19:3–4

Elijah couldn't have run farther. Beersheba was the southern limit of the land. And once there, he bored deeply into the wilderness—another full day's walk—until he stumbled and fell in exhaustion under a tree.

Now, the question is, why? Why did Elijah fear Jezebel's intimidating threats? Why did he run away from his longstanding priority of serving God and hide in fear under the shadow of that solitary tree, deep in the wilderness?

First, Elijah was not thinking realistically or clearly.

Elijah was so shortsighted that he failed to consider the source of this threat. Think about it. The threat hadn't come from God; it had come from an unbelieving, carnal human being who lived her godless life light years from the things of God. If Elijah had been thinking clearly and realistically, he would have realized this. His good judgment, as well as his faith, would have provided this kind of self-talk: *"Hey, God is in control here, not Jezebel. Don't give a second thought to her threats. Trust God as you've done for years."*

My dad taught me a simple principle as I was growing up: "Son, when a mule kicks you, don't let it bother you. Just consider the source." When you are kicked by a carnal person, just consider the source. Elijah could have and should have, but he didn't. He wasn't thinking clearly and realistically.

Instead of praying, "Lord, I'm feeling myself drawn into this fearful thing; I ask You for strength right now," he caved in and ran for cover.

Second, Elijah separated himself from strengthening relationships.

The Scripture says he "left his servant," and "he himself" went alone "a day's journey into the wilderness."

Discouraged people are lonely people. A juniper tree deep in the wilderness has room for only one underneath it. Beneath the barren branches of discouragement and loneliness there is little shade.

Elijah should have stayed with a trusted friend or comrade who could have pumped encouragement, strength, and objectivity into him. That is one of the best things he could have done. That courage transfusion would have kept him strong. But it's interesting how human nature works. When we get discouraged, the first thing we tend to do is to get alone. And that's often the worst thing we can do.

Third, Elijah was caught in the backwash of a great victory.

Our most vulnerable moments usually come after a great victory, especially if that victory is a mountaintop experience with God. Those are the times when we need to set up a defense against the enemy.

I'm not a rock climber, nor do I enjoy heights. But I find those who are fascinating to watch. I've had several of them tell me that climbing to the peak is often a grueling, exhausting experience, but the anticipation connected with reaching the top gives you incredible determination and heightens your motivation. And once you've arrived, words cannot describe the elation. But *then* comes the greatest challenge: descending the slope. You tend to be a little deflated emotionally, vulnerable to risks, and even a bit careless in unguarded moments.

All this provides an analogy worth remembering in the spiritual realm, which I'm convinced partly explains Elijah's vulnerability. The big battle on Carmel was past. The great victory was only a memory. His energy and emotions had peaked and begun to slide. Had he set in motion a plan to meet any counter-assault (surely he knew that the wholesale slaughter of all those prophets and priests would incite the rage of Ahab and Jezebel), Elijah would have been ready for anything. But since he didn't do that, he was vulnerable and he got caught in the backwash.

Fourth, Elijah was physically exhausted and emotionally spent.

For years Elijah had lived on the edge. He was a wanted and hunted man, considered by the king to be Public Enemy Number One. Furthermore, for many of those years he had been roughing it in the wilderness, close to starvation. On the heels of that, he'd had an unbelievable confrontation with the people of Israel, the priests of Asherah, and the prophets of Baal. There is little doubt that Elijah had come to the end of his rope physically and, for sure, emotionally—all of which couldn't help but weaken him spiritually.

There is an old Greek saying: "You will break the bow if you keep it always bent." In other words, if you're living under constant, relentless stress, you'll finally break under the pressure. You have to give yourself some time for rest and refreshment.

For years I've seen evidence of this in my own life and the lives of my ministerial colleagues. You shouldn't be surprised to discover that pastors tend to get discouraged on Mondays. All week long we are building toward Sunday; it is usually the high point of our week. We've studied and prayed and prepared our sermons. We've counseled and dealt with the needs of our congregation. Sunday comes and it's like an emotional climax where everything comes together. It is *wonderful* (well, usually). Then comes Monday, the down slope of the spiritual mountain, when we are weary and vulnerable to discouragement. (Especially since Monday is also the day when people tend to call about all the things they didn't like on Sunday. Why do you think we usually take Mondays off?)

There is some encouragement in knowing that our battle with the blues is not just a present-day malady. One of my all-time favorite preachers of the past is the colorful Charles Haddon Spurgeon. What a remarkably gifted and powerful servant of God! I've worn out my first copy of his outstanding volume, *Lectures to My Students,* in which he devotes an entire chapter to what he calls "The Minister's Fainting Fits." In it he tells of his own struggle with this problem of discouragement . . . sometimes even depression.

Here are several excerpts from Spurgeon's observations and admissions:

The times most favourable to fits of depression, so far as I have experienced, may be summed up in a brief catalogue. First among them I must mention *the hour of great success.* When at last a long-cherished desire is fulfilled, when God has been glorified greatly by our means, and a great triumph achieved, then we are apt to faint. It might be imagined that amid special favours our soul would soar to heights of ecstacy, and rejoice with joy unspeakable, but it is generally the reverse. The Lord seldom exposes His warriors to the perils of exultation over victory; he knows that few of them can endure such a test, and therefore dashes their cup with bitterness. . . .

Excess of joy or excitement must be paid for by subsequent depressions. While the trial lasts, the strength is equal to the emergency; but when it is over, natural weakness claims the right to show itself. . . .

Before any great achievement, some measure of the same depression is very usual. Surveying the difficulties before us, our hearts sink within us. . . . Such was my experience when I first became a pastor in London. My success appalled me; and the thought of the career which it seemed to open up, so far from elating me, cast me into the lowest depth, out of which I uttered my *miserere* and found no room for a *gloria in excelsis.* Who was I that I should continue to lead so great a multitude? I would betake me to my village obscurity, or emigrate to America, and find a solitary nest in the backwoods, where I might be sufficient for the things which would be demanded of me. It was just then that the curtain was rising upon my life-work, and I dreaded what it might reveal. . . .

Let no man who looks for ease of mind and seeks the quietude of life enter the ministry; if he does so he will flee from it in disgust.[1]

I don't know if Elijah was disgusted, but I can tell you he was exhausted. You can hear it in his words: "It is enough; now, O Lord, take my life, for I am not better than my fathers."

Fifth, Elijah got lost in self-pity.

Self-pity is a pathetic emotion. It will lie to you. It will exaggerate. It will drive you to tears. It will cultivate a "victim mentality" in your head. And, in the worst-case scenario, it can bring you to the point of wishing to die, which is exactly where Elijah was.

He said, "For I am not better than my fathers."

Who ever said he had to be? Nobody told him that he had to be better than his fathers. He told himself that!

We open the door for that pathetic liar, self-pity, when we establish an unrealistic standard and then can't live up to it. Self-pity mauls its way inside our minds like a beast and claws us to shreds.

Let's allow God to set our standard. He is always loving, always affirming, always accepting, always faithful to uphold us.

And it was the faithful Jehovah God who now stepped on the scene after Ahab, Jezebel, and Elijah had played their parts in this unfolding drama.

> And he lay down and slept under a juniper tree; and behold, there was an angel touching him, and he said to him, "Arise, eat."
>
> Then he looked and behold, there was at his head a bread cake baked on hot stones, and a jar of water. So he ate and drank and lay down again.
>
> And the angel of the LORD came again a second time and touched him and said, "Arise, eat, because the journey is too great for you."
>
> So he arose and ate and drank, and went in the strength of that food forty days and forty nights to Horeb, the mountain of God.
>
> 1 Kings 19:5–8

God met his servant, Elijah, in his desperate moment of discouragement and despair. This is mercy at its best, beautifully portrayed by the Master Himself.

First, God allowed Elijah a time of rest and refreshment. No sermon. No rebuke. No blame. No shame. No lightning bolt from heaven, saying, "Look at you! Get up, you worthless ingrate! Get on your feet! Quickly, back on the job!"

Instead, God said, "Take it easy, my son. Relax. You haven't had a good meal in a long time." Then He catered a meal of freshly baked bread and cool, refreshing water. That must have brought back sweet memories of those simple days by the brook at Cherith. How gracious of God!

Exhaustion can make you turn emotional cartwheels. Fatigue can lead to all sorts of strange imaginations. It'll make you believe a lie. Elijah was believing a lie, partly because he was exhausted. So God gave him rest and refreshment, and afterward Elijah went on forty days and nights in the strength of it.

Second, God communicated wisely with Elijah.

> Then he came there to a cave, and lodged there; and behold, the word of the LORD came to him, and He said to him, "What are you doing here, Elijah?"
>
> 1 Kings 19:9

God didn't come to Elijah and say, "You ought to be ashamed of yourself, young man." He didn't say, "Snap out of it, son. You shouldn't feel like this."

Instead, God asked a question—a simple question of clarification: "What are you doing here, Elijah?"

And Elijah came back with his self-pitying whine.

> And he said, "I have been very zealous for the LORD, the God of hosts; for the sons of Israel have forsaken Thy covenant, torn down Thine altars and killed Thy prophets with the sword. And I alone am left; and they seek my life, to take it away."
>
> 1 Kings 19:10

Elijah was believing the big lie: "I'm all alone here. I'm the only voice left for God. And they're trying to kill me!"

But God graciously listened to him. God didn't say, "That's dumb, Elijah. How stupid can you get?" God did not rebuke his despondent prophet.

Instead, God said, "Elijah! Get up and walk out of this cave. Man, it's dark in here. Go out there and stand in the light. Stand on the mountain before Me. That's the place to be encouraged. Forget Jezebel. I want you to get your eyes on Me, Elijah. Come on, I'm here for you. I always will be."

> So He said, "Go forth, and stand on the mountain before the LORD."
> And behold, the LORD was passing by! And a great and strong wind
> was rending the mountains and breaking in pieces the rocks before
> the LORD; but the LORD was not in the wind. And after the wind an
> earthquake, but the LORD was not in the earthquake.
> And after the earthquake a fire, but the LORD was not in the fire; . . .
>
> 1 Kings 19:11–12a

Wind . . . earthquake . . . fire. One right after another. And there stands Elijah in the midst of them, his stained old mantle wrapped around him, waiting before God. But God was not in any of those mighty upheavals.

Then, just as you might expect from the God of all mercy:

> . . . after the fire a sound of a gentle blowing.
> And it came about when Elijah heard it, that he wrapped his face
> in his mantle, and went out and stood in the entrance of the cave.
> And behold, a voice came to him and said, "What are you doing here,
> Elijah?"
>
> 1 Kings 19:12b–13

God's presence was not in wind or earthquake or fire. His voice came in the gentle breeze. Those sweet zephyrs were like windswept, invisible magnets, drawing Elijah out of the cave.

Do you see what God did? He drew Elijah out of the cave of self-pity and discouragement and depression. And once Elijah was out of that cave, God asked him again, "What are you doing here, Elijah?"

Once more Elijah came back with that same self-pitying explanation. But this time God gave His prophet some clarification on how matters really stood.

> And the LORD said to him, "Go, return on your way to the wilderness of Damascus, and when you have arrived, you shall anoint Hazael king over Aram; and Jehu the son of Nimshi you shall anoint king over Israel; and Elisha the son of Shaphat of Abel-meholah you shall anoint as prophet in your place.
>
> "And it shall come about, the one who escapes from the sword of Hazael, Jehu shall put to death, and the one who escapes from the sword of Jehu, Elisha shall put to death.
>
> "Yet I will leave 7,000 in Israel, all the knees that have not bowed to Baal and every mouth that has not kissed him."
>
> 1 Kings 19:15–18

God showed Elijah that he still had a job to do—that there was still a place for him. Disillusioned and exhausted though he was, he was still God's man and God's choice for "such a time as this" (Esther 4:14). And, as far as this I'm-all-alone stuff went . . . "Well, Elijah, let Me set the record straight," said God. "There are seven thousand faithful out there who have not bowed to Baal. You're really not alone. At any given moment, with the snap of My divine fingers, I can bring to the forefront a whole fresh battalion of My troops." What reassurance that brought.

Third, God gave Elijah a close, personal friend.

I love the end of this chapter!

> So he departed from there and found Elisha the son of Shaphat, while he was plowing with twelve pairs of oxen before him, and he with the twelfth. And Elijah passed over to him and threw his mantle on him.
>
> And he left the oxen and ran after Elijah and said, "Please let me kiss my father and my mother, then I will follow you." And he said to him, "Go back again, for what have I done to you?"
>
> So he returned from following him, and took the pair of oxen and sacrificed them and boiled their flesh with the implements of the oxen, and gave it to the people and they ate. Then he arose and followed Elijah and ministered to him.
>
> 1 Kings 19:19–21

Thanks to God's kind and gentle dealing, Elijah crawled out of the cave. "He departed from there." God graciously nurtured him through rest and refreshment, gave him some wise counsel, and made him feel significant again in His plan. Talk about compassion!

Then God allowed Elijah to pass his mantle to Elisha, his successor. But God did more than that, abundantly more. For Elisha "arose and followed Elijah and ministered to him." God not only gave Elijah a successor; He also raised up a close, personal friend—someone who loved Elijah and understood him well enough to minister to him and encourage him.

God has not designed us to live like hermits in a cave. He has designed us to live in friendship and fellowship and community with others. That's why the church, the body of Christ, is so very important, for it is there that we are drawn together in love and mutual encouragement. We're meant to be a part of one another's lives. Otherwise, we pull back, focusing on ourselves—thinking how hard we have it or how unfair others are.

Elijah *had* to get his eyes back on the Lord. That was absolutely essential. He had been used mightily, but it was *the Lord* who made him mighty. He stood strong against the enemy, but it was *the Lord* who had given him the strength.

Often we are more enamored with the gifts God gives us than with the Giver himself. When the Lord brings rest and refreshment, we become more grateful for the rest and refreshment than for the God who allows it. When God gives us a good friend, we become absorbed in that friendship and so preoccupied with the friend that we forget it was our gracious God who gave us the friend. We so easily focus on the wrong things.

Many years ago I called on a man in the Veterans Hospital. He had suffered a series of heart attacks and had undergone major surgery. During his rehabilitation, he stayed at the dismal Veterans Hospital.

The day I arrived to visit, I saw a touching scene. This man had a young son, and during his confinement in the hospital, he had made a little wooden truck for his boy. Since the boy was not allowed to go into the ward and visit his father, an orderly had brought the gift down to the child, who was waiting in front of the hospital with his mother. The father was looking out of a fifth-floor window, watching his son unwrap the gift.

The little boy opened the package and his eyes got wide when he saw that wonderful little truck. He hugged it to his chest.

Meanwhile, the father was walking back and forth waving his arms behind the windowpane, trying to get his son's attention.

The little boy put the truck down and reached up and hugged the orderly and thanked him for the truck. And all the while the frustrated father was going through these dramatic gestures, trying to say, "It's me, son. I made that truck for you. I gave that to you. Look up here!" I could almost read his lips.

Finally the mother and the orderly turned the boy's attention up to that fifth-floor window. It was then the boy cried, "Daddy! Oh, thank you! I miss you, Daddy! Come home, Daddy. Thank you for my truck."

And the father stood in the window with tears pouring down his cheeks.

How much like that child we are. We are shut away in our cave of loneliness and discouragement, and then God brings along the gifts of rest and refreshment, wise counsel, and close, personal friends. And we fall in love with the gifts, rather than the Giver!

He gives us a verse of Scripture, and we worship the Bible rather than the One who gave it. He gives us a loving wife or husband or friend, and we fall more in love with the person than the One who gave us that important individual. He gives us a good job, and we love the job more than we love Him. And all the while He stands at the window and says, "Look up here. I gave that to you." He longs to have us look up and say, "Oh, thank You, Father! I miss You. I want to be with You."

Elijah reminds us to look up.

Let's look up after the Lord graciously delivers us from our depression.

Let's look up when He allows us rest and refreshment following an exhausting schedule that has taken its toll on us.

Let's look up and thank Him when He gently and patiently speaks to us from His Word after we've climbed out of a pit of self-pity.

Let's look up and praise Him when He faithfully provides the companionship and affirmation of a friend who understands and encourages us.

Let's look up and acknowledge the Giver more than the gift.

Let's say, "Thank You, Lord, for telling us all about Elijah," who is an unforgettable example that there is nowhere to look but up.

*Now it came about after these things, that Naboth the Jezreelite had a vine-
yard which was in Jezreel beside the palace of Ahab king of Samaria. And
Ahab spoke to Naboth, saying, "Give me your vineyard, that I may have it for
a vegetable garden because it is close beside my house, and I will give you a
better vineyard than it in its place; if you like, I will give you the price of it in
money." But Naboth said to Ahab, "The LORD forbid me that I should give
you the inheritance of my fathers." So Ahab came into his house sullen and
vexed because of the word which Naboth the Jezreelite had spoken to him; for
he said, "I will not give you the inheritance of my fathers." And he lay down
on his bed and turned away his face and ate no food. But Jezebel his wife came
to him and said to him, "How is it that your spirit is so sullen that you are not
eating food?" So he said to her, "Because I spoke to Naboth the Jezreelite,
and said to him, 'Give me your vineyard for money; or else, if it pleases you, I
will give you a vineyard in its place.' But he said, 'I will not give you my vineyard.'" And Jezebel his wife said to him, "Do you now reign over Israel?
Arise, eat bread, and let your heart be joyful; I will give you the vineyard of
Naboth the Jezreelite." So she wrote letters in Ahab's name and sealed them
with his seal, and sent letters to the elders and to the nobles who were living
with Naboth in his city. Now she wrote in the letters, saying, "Proclaim a fast,
and seat Naboth at the head of the people; and seat two worthless men before
him, and let them testify against him, saying, 'You cursed God and the king.'
Then take him out and stone him to death." So the men of his city, the elders
and the nobles who lived in his city, did as Jezebel had sent word to them, just
as it was written in the letters which she had sent them. They proclaimed a fast
and seated Naboth at the head of the people. Then the two worthless men
came in and sat before him; and the worthless men testified against him, even
against Naboth, before the people, saying, "Naboth cursed God and the king."
So they took him outside the city and stoned him to death with stones. Then
they sent word to Jezebel, saying, "Naboth has been stoned, and is dead." And
it came about when Jezebel heard that Naboth had been stoned and was dead,*

that Jezebel said to Ahab, "Arise, take possession of the vineyard of Naboth, the Jezreelite, which he refused to give you for money; for Naboth is not alive, but dead." And it came about when Ahab heard that Naboth was dead, that Ahab arose to go down to the vineyard of Naboth the Jezreelite, to take possession of it. Then the word of the LORD came to Elijah the Tishbite, saying, "Arise, go down to meet Ahab king of Israel, who is in Samaria; behold, he is in the vineyard of Naboth where he has gone down to take possession of it. And you shall speak to him, saying, 'Thus says the LORD, . . . "In the place where the dogs licked up the blood of Naboth the dogs shall lick up your blood, even yours." ' " And Ahab said to Elijah, "Have you found me, O my enemy?" And he amswered, "I have found you, because you have sold yourself to do evil in the sight of the LORD. Behold, I will bring evil upon you, and will utterly sweep you away, and will cut off from Ahab every male, both bond and free in Israel; and I will make your house like the house of Jeroboam the son of Nebat, and like the house of Baasha the son of Ahijah, because of the provocation with which you have provoked Me to anger, and because you have made Israel sin. And of Jezebel also has the LORD spoken, saying, 'The dogs shall eat Jezebel in the district of Jezreel.' The one belonging to Ahab, who dies in the dity, the dogs shall eat, and the one who dies in the field the birds of heaven shall eat." Surely there was no one like Ahab who sold himself to do evil in the sight of the LORD, because Jezebel his wife incited him. And he acted very abominably in following idols, according to all that the Amorites had done, whom the LORD cast out before the sons of Israel. And it came about when Ahab heard these words, that he tore his clothes and put on sackcloth and fasted, and he lay in sackcloth and went about despondently. Then the word of the LORD came to Elijah the Tishbite, saying, "Do you see how Ahab has humbled himself before Me? Because he has humbled himself before Me, I will not bring the evil in his days, but I will bring the evil upon his house in his son's days."

1 KINGS 21:1–29

Chapter Eight

When God says, "That's enough!"

God is good. From our earliest years of Christian training, we have affirmed the goodness of God. How full of compassion He is! He possesses an infinite capacity of love and mercy, grace and patience. All these traits are immeasurable in Him—beyond our comprehension. We find great comfort in this.

God is also just. In the Scriptures His justice and righteousness are intertwined. In fact, the same original term in the sacred text is often translated either "justice" or "righteousness." We love the fact that God is good and compassionate, but it doesn't sit with us quite as easily that He is just. Nevertheless, it is a dimension of His character that we, as His children, must not overlook.

> God's compassion flows out of His goodness, and goodness without justice is not goodness. God spares us because He is good, but He could not be good if He were not just. . . .
>
> God's justice stands forever against the sinner in utter severity. The value and tenuous hope that God is too kind to punish the ungodly has

become a deadly opiate for the consciences of millions. It hushes their fears and allows them to practice all pleasant forms of iniquity while death draws every day nearer and the command to repent goes unregarded. As responsible moral beings we dare not so trifle with our eternal future.[1]

We enjoy speaking of and celebrating the love of God, and so we should. But there is another side of His character that we cannot deny or ignore, and that is God's wrath. He *is* patient and merciful, compassionate and longsuffering, but His compassion has its limit—and that limit is not insignificant. God can come to the end of His patience, and when He does, it's as if He says, "That is enough!"

Proverbs 29:1 tells us that "A man who hardens his neck after much reproof will suddenly be broken beyond remedy." Look closely at those words. They clearly convey a warning and a promise. In this verse God is revealing the truth about Himself and man, who stubbornly refuses to listen to His voice, relying on the *deadly opiate* to hush his fears.

The term "man" here, of course, addresses mankind in general—men and women. The person in question is one who "hardens his neck." The New International Version translates this "stiff-necked." In other words, this is a person who hears and doesn't respond—a person deafened by his or her own stubborn will. God says that such a person will, after much reproof, "suddenly be broken beyond remedy." A literal rendering would be, "and there is no remedy." This person will suddenly be broken, and there is no remedy. Pause and ponder the severity of those words.

Such statements are rare in Scripture. Often God's pronouncements are followed by offers of His grace and mercy, for He frequently reminds us of His longsuffering, His patience. God understands our make-up. He knows that we are imperfect, and He stands ready and willing to forgive and forget our confessed sins—to reinstate, to reschedule, to confirm. But here there is none of that. This offense has reached the point of no return. It is "beyond remedy." It is terminal. The end. God says, "That is enough! You'll go no farther." That's as serious as it gets.

Another example is found in Proverbs 6:12–15:

> A worthless person, a wicked man,
> Is the one who walks with a false mouth,
> Who winks with his eyes, who signals with his feet,
> Who points with his fingers;
> Who with perversity in his heart devises evil continually,
> Who spreads strife.
> Therefore his calamity will come suddenly;
> Instantly he will be broken, and there will be no healing.

There comes a time when God finally says to those who stubbornly refuse to listen: "You will go no farther. That is all!" When this moment arrives, "his calamity will come suddenly" and "there will be no healing."

THREE EXAMPLES OF DIVINE SEVERITY

We do not play games with God, and God does not play games with us. Let me mention three examples from Scripture.

First, Sodom and Gomorrah. God, with infinite patience and grace and mercy, permitted these cities to exist, until, given the immorality, the debauchery, the perversion, and the moral pollution of their citizens, He reached the limit of His patience. Their stubborn refusal to hear His voice grew to such proportions that God finally said to His servant Abraham, in effect, "That's enough! I will take no more of their unrestrained wickedness!" And suddenly, irrevocably, He rained down fire from heaven, and the cities of Sodom and Gomorrah literally were no more. God's justice came "suddenly," and the consequences were "beyond remedy."

The second example is Herod Agrippa I, to whom God said, in so many words, "That is enough! You will go no farther." The story of Herod's demise is not a happy one, but it is realistic.

> And on an appointed day Herod, having put on his royal apparel, took his seat on the rostrum and began delivering an address to them.
> And the people kept crying out, "The voice of a god and not of a man!"

> And immediately an angel of the Lord struck him because he did not give God the glory, and he was eaten by worms and died.
>
> Acts 12:21–23

The Jewish historian Josephus describes this event in his record. He says that at the time this occurred Herod was dressed in silver-lined garments, and the early-morning sun was reflecting brightly off his garments. As he stood there in all his earthly splendor, the people began calling him a god. And Herod accepted their praise and their worship. That was enough.

Suddenly, Herod was stricken with a terrible pain in his abdomen. He doubled over and had to be carried to his bedchamber. For five days he lived with relentless, agonizing pain until his life was snapped from him. In the brief words of Scripture, "The worms ate him within, and he died."

Herod accepted the worship and praise due only to God. And "because he did not give God the glory," God said, "That's enough!" Suddenly there was "no healing."

Third, God not only loses patience with cities and individuals; He also loses patience with entire nations.

> Zedekiah was twenty-one years old when he became king, and he reigned eleven years in Jerusalem. And he did evil in the sight of the LORD his God; he did not humble himself before Jeremiah the prophet who spoke for the LORD.
>
> And he also rebelled against King Nebuchadnezzar who had made him swear allegiance by God. But he stiffened his neck and hardened his heart against turning to the LORD God of Israel.
>
> Furthermore, all the officials of the priests and the people were very unfaithful following all the abominations of the nations; and they defiled the house of the LORD which He had sanctified in Jerusalem.
>
> And the LORD, the God of their fathers, sent word to them again and again by His messengers, because He had compassion on His people and on His dwelling place; but they continually mocked the messengers of God, despised His words and scoffed at His prophets, until the wrath of the LORD arose against His people, *until there was no remedy.*
>
> 2 Chronicles 36:11–16 [italics added]

For over three hundred years the nation of Judah had been living under one godless monarch after another, rebelling against God and mocking the messengers He sent "because He had compassion on His people." Finally God said, "That is enough. I will tolerate you no longer, Judah." And again, at the termination point of God's patience, we read those haunting words: "No remedy."

God comes to the end of His patience. He can do it with a city. He can do it with an individual. He can do it with a nation. And as we see in this next chapter from Elijah's life, He can do it with a couple: a husband and wife who are partners in sin.

A SPECIFIC EXAMPLE OF DIVINE JUDGMENT

Elijah had been dealing with Ahab and Jezebel since the beginning of his prophetic ministry. Both his message and his model of life were well known to them. For years they were exposed to the truth, and for years God patiently waited. Still, they refused to believe. The powerful showdown on Mount Carmel, where God proved Himself as the One to follow, instead of softening their hearts, only made them harder. They stubbornly and deliberately refused to repent.

In spite of all this exposure to God's miraculous workings, they had "hardened their necks." This godless king and his wife had killed God's prophets and bowed down to Baal. But now things went from bad to worse. Their dealings in this next chapter show how despicable this pair really was.

> Now it came about after these things, that Naboth the Jezreelite had a vineyard which was in Jezreel beside the palace of Ahab king of Samaria.
>
> And Ahab spoke to Naboth, saying, "Give me your vineyard, that I may have it for a vegetable garden because it is close beside my house, and I will give you a better vineyard than it in its place; if you like, I will give you the price of it in money."
>
> 1 Kings 21:1–2

Naboth is a simple man who owns a little piece of ground with a vineyard on it. This vineyard, which Naboth inherited from his father, happens to lie within the shadow of King Ahab's majestic palace. One day, for some twisted reason, Ahab notices it and soon becomes bound and determined to own it.

Perhaps Ahab is bored that day. And as he sits there gazing out the window, he notices Naboth working in his vineyard. *Hmmm,* thinks Ahab. *That looks like a nice patch of land. That would make a good vegetable garden.* So he approaches Naboth and says, "I want that piece of land. I'll give you an even better vineyard in exchange for it. Or I'll pay you for it."

Now according to Jewish law, Naboth could not sell his father's inheritance, and he reminds the king of this.

> But Naboth said to Ahab, "The LORD forbid me that I should give you the inheritance of my fathers."
>
> 1 Kings 21:3

Ahab is not satisfied with this explanation. He has made an offer and it has been legitimately refused. But he is Ahab, king of all Israel. Like a little child, he wants what he wants when he wants it.

> So Ahab came into his house sullen and vexed because of the word which Naboth the Jezreelite had spoken to him; for he said, "I will not give you the inheritance of my fathers." And he lay down on his bed and turned away his face and ate no food.
>
> 1 Kings 21:4

Mind you, this is a grown man (well, he was adult in size). Not only was he a grown man, but the king of the nation of Israel (but not necessarily the power on the throne), and he is pouting like a child who hasn't gotten his way. "Sullen" and "vexed," he goes to his room and slams the door and refuses to eat.

> But Jezebel his wife came to him and said to him, "How is it that your spirit is so sullen that you are not eating food?"
>
> So he said to her, "Because I spoke to Naboth the Jezreelite, and said to him, 'Give me your vineyard for money; or else, if it pleases

you, I will give you a vineyard in its place.' But he said, 'I will not give you my vineyard.' "

And Jezebel his wife said to him, "Do you now reign over Israel? Arise, eat bread, and let your heart be joyful; I will give you the vineyard of Naboth the Jezreelite."

1 Kings 21:5–7

"Do you now reign over Israel?" Jezebel asks her husband. Well, in reality, the answer is no. Jezebel is the reigning authority—just ask *her!* To prove this, when Ahab tells her why he is pouting and not eating, she immediately takes matters into her own hands. "Forget about it," she tells him. "Get up and eat, sweetie. Relax and rejoice. *I'll* get you that vineyard."

Her husband is under stress and pressure. True, it's of his own making, but nevertheless that's where he is. So Jezebel takes over and acts in the flesh. She doesn't step back from the emotion of the moment and evaluate the situation wisely. She doesn't ask God to work in her husband's heart. That's not the way she operates. She is a godless woman who lives her life in the carnality of self-satisfying desires. Her advice reflects that.

"I'll take care of this for you," she says to her husband. "Just get out of my way."

So she wrote letters in Ahab's name and sealed them with his seal, and sent letters to the elders and to the nobles who were living with Naboth in his city.

Now she wrote in the letters, saying, "Proclaim a fast, and seat Naboth at the head of the people; and seat two worthless men before him, and let them testify against him, saying, 'You cursed God and the king.' Then take him out and stone him to death."

1 Kings 21:8–10

Jezebel has no authority to write letters in the king's name. But that is not her worst offense. In writing these letters, she sets in motion a plot to kill Naboth. In today's terms, she "frames" the helpless man. But she makes it appear that she is following the letter of the law.

Although two witnesses were required in capital cases (Deuteronomy 17:5–6), these two were worthless, lowlife scoundrels, easily bribed into giving false testimonies. They fit perfectly in the portrait of disreputable witnesses painted by Solomon in Proverbs 19:28: "A rascally witness makes a mockery of justice, and the mouth of the wicked spreads iniquity." The death of Naboth was an outrageously deceptive act of murder.

> So the men of his city, the elders and the nobles who lived in his city, did as Jezebel had sent word to them, just as it was written in the letters which she had sent them.
>
> They proclaimed a fast and seated Naboth at the head of the people.
>
> Then the two worthless men came in and sat before him; and the worthless men testified against him, even against Naboth, before the people, saying, "Naboth cursed God and the king." So they took him outside the city and stoned him to death with stones.
>
> 1 Kings 21:11–13

It is worth noting that those who cooperated in this scheme were not simply the two worthless men who lied on the stand, but "the elders and the nobles" who went along with Jezebel's instructions. The whole system was corrupt. Justice and integrity were not to be found in this godless administration. No one sought truth. They gave the appearance of being concerned about what was right, but in reality, they were all a pack of liars and murderers.

So they set Naboth up for the kill. He is seated in a place of prominence, probably enjoying himself, thinking how privileged he is to be invited, when suddenly two "scoundrels" (NIV) begin accusing him of terrible acts. "Naboth cursed God and the king," they say. As a result, in a matter of minutes, Naboth is hauled outside the city walls and stoned to death.

> Then they sent word to Jezebel, saying, "Naboth has been stoned, and is dead."
>
> And it came about when Jezebel heard that Naboth had been stoned and was dead, that Jezebel said to Ahab, "Arise, take possession of the vineyard of Naboth, the Jezreelite, which he refused to give you for money; for Naboth is not alive, but dead."

> And it came about when Ahab heard that Naboth was dead, that Ahab arose to go down to the vineyard of Naboth the Jezreelite, to take possession of it.
>
> 1 Kings 21:14–16

Look at Ahab's response. It's predictable. As is his custom, he leans on Jezebel, and she comes through. He never questions how this has come about. He never asks what happened to Naboth. He simply accepts what he has wanted all along: Naboth's vineyard. Without hesitation, he stakes his claim on this piece of land.

Once again, wickedness reigned in Ahab's court. Many of the citizens must have known the truth, but they obviously shrugged their shoulders and looked the other way. You live long enough under the influence of immoral, unethical, and idolatrous leadership, and you're no longer outraged at anything.

But God has come to the end of His patience with this pair. He's put up with years of their godless acts . . . but no longer. As with Sodom and Gomorrah, God says, in effect, "That is enough. You will go no farther."

A FINAL DAY OF JUDGMENT

Elijah has remained out of the picture thus far. It's almost as if God were giving Ahab and Jezebel a final opportunity to turn to Him on their own. No way! They evidenced absolutely no change of heart. Instead, left to themselves, their wicked ways intensified.

So God brings Elijah, His prophet and spokesman, back on the scene. God has had enough. No more promises. No more opportunities for repentance. His wheels of patience have screeched to a halt. It's time for justice and judgment.

> Then the word of the LORD came to Elijah the Tishbite, saying,
>
> Arise, go down to meet Ahab king of Israel, who is in Samaria; behold, he is in the vineyard of Naboth where he has gone down to take possession of it.

"And you shall speak to him, saying, 'Thus says the LORD, "Have you murdered, and also taken possession?"' And you shall speak to him, saying, 'Thus says the LORD, "In the place where the dogs licked up the blood of Naboth the dogs shall lick up your blood, even yours."'"

1 Kings 21:17–19

That's how justice sounds when God reaches the end of His tether. It isn't a pleasant message. It doesn't sound compassionate, nor should it. Never being one to argue with God or second-guess His mandates, Elijah listened, accepted the plan, and obeyed his Lord. Faithful messengers tell the truth, whether it's about God's love or a message of divine judgment.

And Ahab said to Elijah, "Have you found me, O my enemy?" And he answered, "I have found you, because you have sold yourself to do evil in the sight of the LORD."

1 Kings 21:20

What an opening line! There is no doubt in Ahab's mind that enmity exists between him and God's prophet. Elijah doesn't deny this, nor does he beat around the bush; he comes right to the point. A final rebuke is in order.

The Hebrew word that is translated "sold yourself" also conveys the idea of habitual, constant activity—trafficking in wickedness. Interestingly, it can also mean "to marry." That's an insightful wordplay on Elijah's part, in light of the relationship between Ahab and Jezebel. Ahab had married an evil woman, and in doing so, he had also married himself to the dark realm of evil. He had embraced it in every area of his life as a result of taking Jezebel as his life's partner.

God had waited patiently. No change. He had sent His prophet to warn Ahab and Jezebel over and over again. No change. Finally, His patience was exhausted. "That is enough!" God said through His spokesman Elijah. "No remedy."

Please read with care the solemn pronouncement of judgment upon Ahab and Jezebel which Elijah fearlessly delievered:

"Behold, I will bring evil upon you, and will utterly sweep you away, and will cut off from Ahab every male, both bond and free in Israel; and I will make your house like the house of Jeroboam the son of Nebat, and like the house of Baasha the son of Ahijah, because of the provocation with which you have provoked Me to anger, and because you have made Israel sin.

"And of Jezebel also has the LORD spoken, saying, 'The dogs shall eat Jezebel in the district of Jezreel.'

"The one belonging to Ahab, who dies in the city, the dogs shall eat, and the one who dies in the field the birds of heaven shall eat."

1 Kings 21:21–24

Like Nathan before guilt-ridden King David, Elijah stands before wicked King Ahab. With penetrating eyes the prophet looks deep into the man's depraved soul and delivers the goods. Judgment is coming. Doom is sure. Death is imminent.

Elijah "was a Mount-Sinai of a man, with a heart like a thunderstorm," writes Alexander Whyte, and never more so than at this epochal moment of confrontation. Ahab must have broken out in a cold sweat. God had spoken. Hell was nearer than it had ever been in his life, and there would be no escaping its awful fury.

After recording these dire predictions, spoken by the Lord through Elijah, the writer of 1 Kings gives this commentary on the lives of Ahab and Jezebel:

Surely there was no one like Ahab who sold himself to do evil in the sight of the LORD, because Jezebel his wife incited him.

And he acted very abominably in following idols, according to all that the Amorites had done, whom the LORD cast out before the sons of Israel.

1 Kings 21:25–26

What a partnership! They were partners in unparalleled evil, until God finally said, "That's enough."

TWO SOLEMN REMINDERS

Here are two sobering and solemn reminders for us to consider:

1. There is an end to God's patience. No one knows it.

God's wheels grind slowly but exceedingly fine. God, in gracious patience and mercy, waits for us to hear His voice and obey. People hear the Gospel of salvation and do not respond. Yet God waits. Some claim His name, but live in a way that says otherwise. Still God waits.

God's patience sometimes even frustrates us, particularly when evil persists, and He doesn't step in and stop it. At times like that, it's easy to convince ourselves that evil goes perpetually unnoticed. Solomon writes of this:

> Because the sentence against an evil deed is not executed quickly, therefore the hearts of the sons of men among them are given fully to do evil.
>
> Ecclesiastes 8:11

What a clear revelation of the excuses people use to stay away from God's conviction, excusing wrong on the basis of delayed punishment. "Well, nothing has happened so far, so I'm still safe." When they get away with a series of sins and see no immediate consequences, they think, *"Aaah! Everything's okay! Hey, I'm safe!"* But that could very well be the last day they'll get away with it.

You and I do not know at what point God reaches His divine limit and says, "That is enough! That's all! I will tolerate this no longer." But I know from this passage and others in Scripture, and I know from His dealings with Sodom and Gomorrah, Herod Agrippa, Ahab and Jezebel that God's patience can and does, finally, run out. Don't be fooled into thinking that His longsuffering is *everlasting* suffering.

2. God keeps His word. No one stops it.

Never forget what you've read in this chapter. Ahab and Jezebel were so powerful, so intimidating, so wicked. They thought they were in charge of everything—invincible. But when God stepped in, it was curtains for them. They were helpless to stop His judgment.

Another powerful monarch offers this same lesson. His name was Belshazzar, and he ruled in the days of the prophet Daniel. Belshazzar, too, was powerful and impressive. And he, too, made the mistake of ignoring God's voice. "Eat, drink, and be merry!" was his motto. Then one night he looked up and saw the hand of God writing across a plastered wall: "I have weighed you on my scales of judgment and I have found you deficient. I am going to put an end to you and to your kingdom" (Daniel 5). Once again God said, "That's enough!" And *that very night* Belshazzar was condemned. He could do *nothing* to stop God's judgment.

If you are a child of God, He will not cast you out of His family. But if you are stubbornly refusing to obey Him, continuing to walk your own way, He will bring severe discipline upon you. He loves you too much to ignore your actions. God can quickly remove you from this earth or take from you the joy of your life. He may even, as He did with the Corinthians, siphon your strength and health so that you become weak and sickly. Some of them, tragically, died due to their carnality.

Our tendency is to compare ourselves to others and say, "Well, I'm not as bad as Jezebel and Ahab." Or to procrastinate and say, "Right now it's too painful. I'll take care of it next week." I plead with you, don't use either one of those foolish excuses—comparison or procrastination. The devil's sharpest tool is delay.

I close with these serious warnings: Don't play games with God. Don't walk away from Him with a stubborn will. For in the end, remember, He always wins. When He says, "That's enough," it's too late.

God is good, and He is also just. And when His justice finally kicks in, there's no escaping it. If you think otherwise, you've bought into "a deadly opiate."

Now Moab rebelled against Israel after the death of Ahab. And Ahaziah fell through the lattice in his upper chamber which was in Samaria, and became ill. So he sent messengers and said to them, "Go, inquire of Baal-zebub, the god of Ekron, whether I shall recover from this sickness." But the angel of the LORD said to Elijah the Tishbite, "Arise, go up to meet the messengers of the king of Samaria and say to them, 'Is it because there is no God in Israel that you are going to inquire of Baal-zebub, the god of Ekron?' Now therefore thus says the LORD, 'You shall not come down from the bed where you have gone up, but you shall surely die.'" Then Elijah departed. When the messengers returned to him he said to them, "Why have you returned?" And they said to him, "A man came up to meet us and said to us, 'Go, return to the king who sent you and say to him, "Thus says the Lord, 'Is it because there is no God in Israel that you are sending to inquire of Baal-zebub, the god of Ekron? Therefore you shall not come down from the bed where you have gone up, but shall surely die.'"'" And he said to them, "What kind of man was he who came up to meet you and spoke these words to you?" And they answered him, "He was a hairy man with a leather girdle bound about his loins." And he said, "It is Elijah the Tishbite." Then the king sent to him a captain of fifty with his fifty. And he went up to him, and behold, he was sitting on the top of the hill. And he said to him, "O man of God, the king says, 'Come down.'" And Elijah answered and said to the captin of fifty, "If I am a man of God, let fire come down from heaven and consume you and your fifty." Then fire came down from heaven and consumed him and his fifty. So he again sent to him another captain of fifty with his fifty. And he answered and said to him, "O man of God, thus says the king, 'Come down quickly.'" And Elijah answered and said to them, "If I am a man of God, let fire come down from heaven and consume you and your fifty." Then the fire of God came down from heaven and consumed him and his fifty. So he again sent the captain of a third fifty with his fifty. When the third captain of the fifty went up, he came and bowed down on his knees before Elijah, and begged him and said to him, "O man of God, please let my life and the lives of these fifty servants of yours be precious in your sight. Behold fire came down from heaven, and consumed the first two captains of fifty with their fifties; but now let my life be precious in your sight." And the angel of the LORD said to Elijah, "Go down with him; do not be afraid of him." So he arose and went down with him to the king. Then he said to him, "Thus says the LORD, 'Because you have sent messengers to inquire of Baal-zebub, the god of Ekron—is it because there is no God in Israel to inquire of His word?—therefore you shall not come down from the bed where you have gone up, but shall surely die.'" So Ahaziah died according to the word of the LORD which Elijah had spoken. And because he had no son, Jehoram became king in his place in the second year of Jehoram the son of Jehoshaphat, king of Judah. Now the rest of the acts of Ahaziah which he did, are they not written in the Book of the Chronicles of the Kings of Israel?

2 KINGS 1:1–18

CHAPTER NINE

Watch Out for the Enemy

I'm sitting here in my study looking at one of those editorial cartoons with a clever but penetrating title, "The Problem with Pedestals." In the center of the picture stands an enormously high pedestal, several stories tall. A ladder is leaning against it with a man near the top getting ready to step off the ladder and onto the top of the pedestal. From my vantage point, as the reader, I can see that the pedestal has a huge target painted on the top of its flat surface, with an oversized bull's-eye right in the center. Off to the side of the target is a sign containing these instructions:

Congratulations!
Please stand still so everyone can get a clean shot
at knocking you down.

Anyone who has been involved in leadership, especially spiritual leadership, knows the truth of that cartoon. After making your way up the ladder, it only seems natural that you should climb onto that pedestal at the top. The applause that accompanies your accomplishment tells you that you've arrived. You deserve to be admired for all your effort and dedication. After all, climbing that ladder wasn't easy.

But once you step onto that elevated plateau of fame, watch out! As the cartoon illustrates, you are now the target of public attention, and knocking you down becomes the name of the game for many (more than you want to believe). This attack is made easier by the fact that up there the gale-force winds of temptation can howl fiercely. Personal blind spots increase. Feelings of indispensability and self-sufficiency can replace a wholesome dependence on the One who has blessed you beyond measure.

Years ago, I committed these wise words to memory:

> No one need aspire to leadership in the work of God who is not prepared to pay a price greater than his contemporaries and colleagues are willing to pay. True leadership always extracts a heavy toll on the whole man, and the more effective the leadership is, the higher the price to be paid.[1]

Elijah lived most of his life in the center of the bull's-eye. Once he delivered God's unwelcome message to the king and the lengthy drought began to take its toll, Elijah's name became a household word all across the land of Israel. He was famous . . . but not popular. Everybody—especially the king—wanted to get their hands on this strange seer who had come out of nowhere, wreaking havoc on their lives.

Elijah's heroic and successful showdown with the prophets and priests of Baal and Asherah on Mount Carmel only intensified his enemies' determination to knock him off the pedestal of invincibility. Enough was enough. No man should have that much power.

God intervened and delivered Elijah from who knows how many traps that had been laid for him. As we just saw in the previous chapter, both Ahab and Jezebel finally went too far, and God ultimately finished them off rather swiftly. Just as God had predicted, Ahab died.

> So the king [Ahab] died and was brought to Samaria, and they buried the king in Samaria.
>
> And they washed the chariot by the pool of Samaria, and the dogs licked up his blood (now the harlots bathed themselves there), according to the word of the LORD which He spoke. . . .

So Ahab slept with his fathers, and Ahaziah his son became king
in his place. . . .

Ahaziah the son of Ahab became king over Israel in Samaria in the
seventeenth year of Jehoshaphat king of Judah, and he reigned two
years over Israel.

And he did evil in the sight of the LORD and walked in the way of
his father and in the way of his mother and in the way of Jeroboam
the son of Nebat, who caused Israel to sin.

So he served Baal and worshiped him and provoked the LORD
God of Israel to anger according to all that his father had done.

1 Kings 22:37–38, 40, 51–53

Ahab's death did not mean, however, that all was well in the land. His son
Ahaziah, most likely his eldest son, succeeded him. As you might imagine,
the son was just like his father, and so for the two years that he ruled,
Ahaziah "did evil in the sight of the Lord." Cut from the same piece of
cloth as his father and his mother, he served Baal.

We know little else about Ahaziah except that he had an accident at
home from which he never fully recovered.

And Ahaziah fell through the lattice in his upper chamber which was
in Samaria, and became ill. So he sent messengers and said to them,
"Go, inquire of Baal-zebub, the god of Ekron, whether I shall recover
from this sickness."

2 Kings 1:2

We are not given the details of Ahaziah's accident. Perhaps he broke a leg or
injured his back or damaged an internal organ in the fall. Maybe he became paralyzed. The narrative does not tell us; it does not even tell us how
far Ahaziah fell. All we know is that the fall led to some serious injury or
illness which, in turn, resulted in an intriguing series of events. And those
events impacted the life of Elijah, who was still the target of his enemies.
Only this time, the enemy was a supernatural foe: Baal-zebub, the god of
Ekron.

When the injured reigning king, Ahaziah, realized he wasn't recovering, he got worried. Having been trained by his parents to handle such complications in life by consulting pagan deities, he sought counsel from the god of Ekron, Baal-zebub by name, hoping the god would tell him if he would recover from his injury. Ekron was one of the five major Philistine cities, a city known for its practice of divination (1 Samuel 5:10, 6:2; Isaiah 2:6), and apparently the god was housed there.

Linguistically the name "Baal-zebub" is a combination of two Hebrew words. *Baal* means "lord or god." *Zebub* is from the verb *zabab*, which means "to dangle, to move here and there quickly." In noun form it means "fly." Together the two words mean "god of the fly" or "lord of the fly."

Old Testament scholars have different theories about what this name meant. Perhaps the statue of the god was formed in the shape of a fly. Maybe it meant a god of medicine or a god that brought relief from the torment and plagues of flies common in the lands of the East. All we know is that this "fly god" was housed at Ekron and, speaking through its seers and witches, predicted the future. That's why Ahaziah sought information from Baal-zebub.

The only time the name Baal-zebub appears in the Old Testament is in this chapter, where it appears four times. In all four places it refers to the same false deity, the god of Ekron. The name does appear again, however, in the New Testament, in the Greek form, Beelzebul.

> Then there was brought to Him [Jesus] a demon-possessed man who was blind and dumb, and He healed him, so that the dumb man spoke and saw.
>
> And all the multitudes were amazed, and began to say, "This man cannot be the Son of David, can he?"
>
> But when the Pharisees heard it, they said, "This man casts out demons only by Beelzebul the ruler of the demons."
>
> Matthew 12:22–24

One of the acts that had been prophesied of Messiah was that He would deliver people from satanic, supernatural power. So the multitudes that followed Jesus were stunned when they saw this son of a carpenter delivering people from the demonic powers of the evil one. *"Could this be the Messiah?"* they wondered. *"Could this be the Son of David?"*

But the Pharisees dismissed this possibility, crediting Jesus' power to "Beelzebul, the ruler of demons."

Now we cannot say for certain that this Beelzebul refers specifically to Satan. The name could refer to one of the princes of demons who have charge over realms of the demonic world. But we know for sure that this Beelzebul is closely related to the Baal-zebub of 2 Kings. Both represent a source of demonic power.

Thus, the god worshiped in Ekron, Baal-zebub, this "lord of the fly," was directly linked with the satanic world of the demons.

When my brother Orville was young, he was interested in science. The scientific project that resulted in his winning the Bausch and Lomb Award when he graduated from high school involved his raising *drosophila melinagasters*. What is a *drosophila melinagaster?* It is the scientific name of a fruit fly. And you have never seen anything multiply like fruit flies that are fed super-ripe bananas and left alone. One night one of the jars somehow got opened, and we had *drosophila melinagasters* all over our house. (Catching them is another story, absolutely hilarious, which no one can tell better than our sister, Luci. So I'll not go there.)

Flies, whether they are fruit flies or houseflies, are pesky, irritating insects, which tells me a great deal about the tormenting power of Baal-zebub and the swarming, misery-making problem created by this kind of god.

Of course Ahaziah, in seeking to know his own future, cared little about the source of the power he was accessing. Like his parents, he was wicked to the core. All he cared about was knowing the future, and to do that he willingly plugged into the power of Baal-zebub.

Some might say, as they certainly did in Elijah's day, "Aw, what's the harm? That god is just a piece of stone or wood. It's not alive." And that may be true, as far as the object itself goes. But the problem has to do with what that object represents, and especially what it does to the idol worshiper. To be sure, the idol itself is just a piece of matter, but through the act of worship it becomes a point of residence for the demonic world. This object that is worshiped, consulted, and sacrificed to is nothing in and of itself, but it can become the breeding ground for the whole world of demonic powers.

Paul, in writing to the Corinthians many centuries later, verifies this:

> What do I mean then? That a thing sacrificed to idols is anything, or that an idol is anything? No, but I say that the things which the Gentiles sacrifice, they sacrifice to demons, and not to God; and I do not want you to become sharers in demons.
>
> 1 Corinthians 10:19–20

On the surface, Baal-zebub was nothing more than a hunk of stone or a chunk of wood, shaped perhaps in the form of a fly, but from it emanated all sorts of supernatural, demonic-inspired abilities, one of which was to tell the future. That is why God stepped in when Ahaziah sent his messenger to consult the god of Ekron.

FACING THE ENEMY HEAD-ON

God intervened. And as we would expect, He used His servant in the process.

> But the angel of the LORD said to Elijah the Tishbite, "Arise, go up to meet the messengers of the king of Samaria and say to them, 'Is it because there is no God in Israel that you are going to inquire of Baal-zebub, the god of Ekron?'
>
> "Now therefore thus says the LORD, 'You shall not come down from the bed where you have gone up, but you shall surely die.'"
> Then Elijah departed.
>
> 2 Kings 1:3–4

God quickly dispatched His prophet to the scene to intercept Ahaziah's messengers. God did not want them to have any contact with the demon-inspired god at Ekron. "Don't let them make that journey!" God said to Elijah. "Stop them! And you ask them, 'Is there no God that you can call upon? Why must you go to this god in Ekron?'"

God moves in swiftly, doesn't He? Here's Ahaziah, confined to his bed, not recovering, wanting to know his future. And the Lord steps in and says, "You tell Ahaziah that his very act, the very decision he has made to consult this false god, will result in terminal illness. He'll never get better."

Well, when the messengers returned and told the king about the man who had intercepted them and the message he had given them, Ahaziah asked one question:

> And he said to them, "What kind of man was he who came up to meet you and spoke these words to you?"
>
> And they answered him, "He was a hairy man with a leather girdle bound about his loins." And he said, "It is Elijah the Tishbite."
>
> 2 Kings 1:7–8

I told you the prophet was notorious. He's standing in the bull's-eye. Ahaziah knew *exactly* who Elijah was. He had heard all about this thorn-in-the-flesh prophet from his mother and father. Elijah had been the restraint on *their* wicked rule, and now here he was again, hounding their son.

But Ahaziah, being like his parents, immediately drew the weapon of intimidation, trying to overwhelm the prophet.

> Then the king sent to him [Elijah] a captain of fifty with his fifty. And he went up to him, and behold, he was sitting on the top of the hill. And he said to him, "O man of God, the king says, 'Come down.'"
>
> And Elijah answered and said to the captain of fifty, "If I am a man of God, let fire come down from heaven and consume you and your fifty." Then fire came down from heaven and consumed him and his fifty.
>
> 2 Kings 1:9–10

Never one to allow the enemy a foothold, Elijah acted quickly. And God honored his servant's refusal to be intimidated.

> So he [the king] again sent to him another captain of fifty with his fifty. And he answered and said to him, "O man of God, thus says the king, 'Come down quickly.'"

> And Elijah answered and said to them, "If I am a man of God, let fire come down from heaven and consume you and your fifty." Then the fire of God came down from heaven and consumed him and his fifty.
>
> 2 Kings 1:11–12

Again, refusing to mess around with soldiers under the command of a wicked ruler, the prophet called down God's judgment. And word traveled swiftly back to the barracks: The hairy man on the mountain was not someone to take lightly!

This third captain was no fool. Notice what he did:

> When the third captain of fifty went up, he came and bowed down on his knees before Elijah, and begged him and said to him, "O man of God, please let my life and the lives of these fifty servants of yours be precious in your sight.
>
> "Behold fire came down from heaven, and consumed the first two captains of fifty with their fifties; but now let my life be precious in your sight."

At that point, the Lord spoke through His angel, giving clear instructions.

> And the angel of the LORD said to Elijah, "Go down with him; do not be afraid of him." So he arose and went down with him to the king.
>
> Then he said to him, "Thus says the LORD, 'Because you have sent messengers to inquire of Baal-zebub, the god of Ekron—is it because there is no God in Israel to inquire of His word?—therefore you shall not come down from the bed where you have gone up, but shall surely die.' "
>
> 2 Kings 1:15–16

Fearlessly, Elijah confronts Ahaziah face to face. This must have reminded him of those times in days past when he had confronted Ahaziah's father, Ahab.

We cannot help but admire Elijah's consistent heroism. The man is alone, standing before the younger king and, surely, surrounded by armed warriors, faithful to Ahaziah, who could have finished him off with one thrust of a spear. Yet God's man never gave the risk a second thought. He was *so* convinced, *so* committed to his Lord, that the thought of self-protection never entered his mind.

As a result, the Lord God, through his courageous spokesman, rebuked Ahaziah for substituting a false source of information (Baal-zebub) for the true source of information (the Lord God of Israel). Listen again to Elijah's piercing question: "Is there no God in Israel that you must seek help from this god of Ekron?" He asked that, fully aware that Ahaziah was a card-carrying idolater. Then Elijah pronounced God's final sentence: "Because you have turned to this false deity, you will never recover, but shall surely die." No remedy.

> So he died, according to the word of the LORD that Elijah had spoken.
>
> 2 Kings 1:17a

The heroism of godly men and women is demonstrated in their being willing to face unpleasant conditions, even threatening circumstances, with remarkable calm. They act with firm resolve, even though it means incurring personal unpopularity. Nothing deters their passion to obey their God . . . regardless. *His* message is paramount. Period.

Few in the history of the church possessed this quality of passionate heroism in greater measure than Martin Luther. It's been asserted that he was, perhaps, as fearless a man as ever lived. "You can expect from me everything save fear or recantation. I shall not flee, much less recant," said Luther on his momentous journey to Worms.

Luther's friends were concerned for his safety. Focusing on the grave dangers ahead, they sought to dissuade him. But the mere thought of *not going* disgusted him. "Not go to Worms!" he said. "I shall go to Worms though there were as many devils as tiles on the roofs."

On a later occasion, while awaiting an audience before all the prelates of the church, Luther was asked if he were now afraid. "Afraid? Greater than the pope and all his cardinals, I fear most that great pope, *self.*"[2]

Amy Carmichael once poetically described this very struggle in her own life:

> God, harden me against myself,
>   The coward with pathetic voice
>   Who craves for ease and rest and joy.
> Myself, arch-traitor to myself,
>   My hollowest friend,
>   My deadliest foe,
>   My clog, whatever road I go.[3]

Elijah rose above his enemies, his king, even himself as he heroically stood his ground, delivered God's message, and refused to dull its edge. May the man's tribe increase in this day of shallow, feel-good theology so popular among superficial, backslapping ministries.

STRAIGHT TALK REGARDING ENEMY TERRITORY

Today, countless people seek to know the future. Newspapers and magazines carry horoscope columns. Television networks advertise psychic hotlines. Bus stop benches boast ads for palm readers. Magazine racks beside grocery store checkout counters offer paperback books on astrology, horoscopes, and other occult subjects. Catalogs carry Ouija boards. The Internet provides a vast array of merchandise for people who are curious about securing information about their fortune and their future.

To many, this hype may sound like sheer silliness; it may appear to be nothing more than harmless fun. After all, what's so bad about reading your daily horoscope? But this is enemy territory. It is anything but silliness or harmless fun. Like the wood and stone idols of Ekron, these present-day seers are substitutes for putting our trust in the living God. And those who look to them to know the future are seeking information from sources that are tied in with a present-day "lord of the flies." How happy the demonic forces are to download their exotic powers into your mind.

God is displeased with any occult involvement. No matter what the motive, no matter how great the need, dabbling with the occult is sin. Remember how swiftly and how totally God dealt with Ahaziah?

God's Word is crystal clear on this subject. Far back in the Book of Leviticus, God gives His people this direct command:

> "Do not turn to mediums or seek out spiritists, for you will be defiled by them. I am the LORD your God."
>
> Leviticus 19:31

When you seek out a medium or a psychic, you become defiled. You become mentally contaminated, emotionally confused, spiritually corrupted. That is not be your intention, but that is the result. Playing off our humanly curious nature, the forces of darkness drop entertaining and innocent-sounding bait. But to take the bait is to compromise your spiritual protection. Whoever moves into this realm opens doors that cannot later be shut. Divine assistance exits as defiling impurities enter in.

> "I will set my face against the person who turns to mediums and spiritists to prostitute himself by following them, and I will cut him off from his people."
>
> Leviticus 20:6

Those are harsh words, but they reveal just how seriously God views the occult, and how harshly He deals with those who have dealings with any form of it.

Before the Israelites ever entered the land that God had promised to them, Moses gave them this mandate and warning:

> When you enter the land the LORD your God is giving you, do not learn to imitate the detestable ways of the nations there.
>
> Let no one be found among you who sacrifices his son or daughter in the fire, who practices divination or sorcery, interprets omens, engages in witchcraft, or casts spells, or who is a medium or spiritist or who consults the dead.

Anyone who does these things is detestable to the LORD, and because of these detestable practices the LORD your God will drive out those nations before you.

Deuteronomy 18:9–12

The *Living Bible* puts it this way:

For example, any Israeli who presents his child to be burned to death as a sacrifice to heathen gods must be killed. No Israeli may practice black magic, or call on the evil spirits for aid, or be a fortune teller, or be a serpent charmer, medium, or wizard, or call forth the spirits of the dead.

Anyone doing these things is an object of horror and disgust to the Lord, and it is because the nations do these things that the Lord your God will displace them.

Deuteronomy 18:10–12

Because the Hebrews did not completely rid the land of all the Canaanites after they took possession, these practices continued. They were even tolerated by those who had been commanded to scour the land of any and all occult activities. And thus the groundwork was laid for the Israelites' own participation in these heathen practices. This demonic-inspired idolatry, which Ahab and Jezebel and their son embraced, originated in those wicked practices that were never driven out of the land centuries earlier.

God is displeased with any occult involvement. Beyond that, *God is dishonored by any specific pursuit of the future that does not find its source in His Word.*

I realize that most people who begin dabbling in astrology or fortune telling or Ouija boards don't take it all that seriously. Astrology, for example, has a captivating appeal. Most do it for fun. Or out of curiosity. But these simple, harmless-looking games begin a process that many cannot handle; and they open doors that should not be opened. Then, it's only a matter of time before the dark powers of demonic forces suck them in, and they find themselves ensnared. As the forces of darkness capture more of their minds, they become driven by these powers, consumed by them, ruled by them, rather than governed by God.

Ahaziah, ill and unable to leave his bed after his fall, was susceptible to the siren call of Baal-zebub. In his weakened condition, totally devoid of devotion to God's truth in spiritual matters, he fell prey to the swarming "lord of lies and flies." We can only imagine the torment of his soul as he "died according to the word of the LORD which Elijah had spoken."

God is displeased with any occult involvement. God is dishonored by any specific pursuit of the future that does not find its source in His Word. But let me reassure you, *God is delighted when we trust Him only.* The Lord strengthens those who put their trust in Him.

If we are not grounded in the Word of God and seeking Him daily as our source of strength and knowledge for the future, we, too, can easily fall prey to the lure of the occult. As I said in an earlier chapter, in another context, we do not play games with God. And we also must learn not to play games with the enemy. Being not only "the lord of the flies," he is also "the father of lies." And when he gets you to believe his lies, he seldom loses.

Learn a lasting lesson from Elijah. As you stand strong for the truth, watch out for the enemy. He not only plays dirty; he also plays for keeps.

And it came about when the LORD was about to take up Elijah by a whirlwind to heaven, that Elijah went with Elisha from Gilgal. And Elijah said to Elisha, "Stay here please, for the LORD has sent me as far as Bethel." But Elisha said, "As the LORD lives and as you yourself live, I will not leave you." So they went down to Bethel. Then the sons of the prophets who were at Bethel came out to Elisha and said to him, "Do you know that the LORD will take away your master from over you today?" And he said, "Yes, I know; be still." And Elijah said to him, "Elisha, please stay here, for the LORD has sent me to Jericho." But he said, "As the LORD lives, and as you yourself live, I will not leave you." So they came to Jericho. And the sons of the prophets who were at Jericho approached Elisha and said to him, "Do you know that the LORD will take away your master from over you today?" And he answered, "Yes, I know; be still." Then Elijah said to him, "Please stay here, for the LORD has sent me to the Jordan." And he said, "As the LORD lives, and as you yourself live, I will not leave you." So the two of them went on. Now fifty men of the sons of the prophets went and stood opposite them at a distance, while the two of them stood by the Jordan. And Elijah took his mantle and folded it together and struck the waters, and they were divided here and there, so that the two of them crossed over on dry ground. Now it came about when they had crossed over, that Elijah said to Elisha, "Ask what I shall do for you before I am taken from you." And Elisha said, "Please, let a double portion of your spirit be upon me." And he said, "You have asked a hard thing. Nevertheless, if you see me when I am taken from you, it shall be so for you; but if not, it shall not be so." Then it came about as they were going along and talking, that behold, there appeared a chariot of fire and horses of fire which separated the two of them. And Elijah went up by a whirlwind to heaven. And Elisha saw it and cried out, "My father, my father, the chariots of Israel and its horsemen!" And he saw him no more. Then he took hold of his own clothes and tore them in two pieces. He also took up the mantle of Elijah that fell from him, and returned and stood by the bank of the Jordan. And he took the mantle of Elijah that fell from him, and struck the waters and said, "Where is the LORD, the God of Elijah?" And when he also had struck the waters, they were divided here and there; and Elisha crossed over.

2 KINGS 2:1—14

Chapter Ten

A No-Death Contract

The most influential, most admired adult in my growing-up years was my maternal grandfather, L. O. Lundy of El Campo, Texas. That's a little south Texas town where I was born back in 1934, just a few blocks from where my grandparents lived. Life was simple during those pre-World War II years. Life was also, for me, innocent, secure, and full of dreams. I spent hours with my Granddaddy Lundy, and to this day, I can vividly recall scenes that still bring a smile of contentment to my soul.

Granddaddy owned a small bay cottage down near Palacios, where my fondest childhood memories were spawned. He also owned what we called a "motorboat," with a 30-horsepower Evinrude engine, which he taught me to handle with a fair amount of confidence. That little 16-foot fishing boat took us out into the saltwater bay, where we caught an assortment of fish: speckled trout, sand trout, redfish, croaker, flounder, drum, and, of course, those ever-present, ornery catfish.

My granddaddy and I had many a conversation as we sat on either end of that boat—early in the morning and late in the evening. We laughed together, caught fish together, discussed life together, but mainly, enjoyed each other's company. I didn't know the word back then, but I realize now that those hours resulted in a very special "bonding" between the two of us. But this much I did know: When I grew up, I wanted to be like the man I admired most of all—Judge L. O. Lundy.

To this day, when I'm near the coast and the pungent smell of shrimp and crab is in the air, my thoughts return to those simple times when I found such comfort in my grandfather's presence, such affection in his arms. With him nearby, there was never any need to hurry, and there was always time to talk. And to this day, on very still evenings when the sun is setting, and I am near the sea, I can almost see his chunky frame silhouetted against the sky, his shock of white hair and his gentle smile. If it is quiet enough, I'd swear I can still hear him clear his throat, which he often did. And if I listen hard enough, it's almost possible for me to hear his laugh. I loved him dearly.

One day our end-of-the-boat philosophical discussions took us to the subject of Jesus' return, which led us to talk about death, a subject that I found mysterious and scary. I had a hundred questions, and Granddaddy seemed to have all the answers. All but one of them brought me comfort. It was when he told me that he wanted to die that I suddenly lost interest in fishing.

"What do you mean, Granddaddy?" I asked, staring at him.

"Well, little Charles, I mean I want the full deal," was his answer.

I didn't get it. "What does 'full deal' mean?"

"That means I want to go through death, be put in a casket, have them bury me in the ground, and then I want to know the great experience of resurrection when Jesus comes back."

Then, looking directly at me from his end of the boat, he added with a chuckle, "I want the full load!"

I found that amazing, and a little disturbing—amazing because I had never thought of such a thing, and disturbing because I never wanted my granddaddy to die. The thought of ever seeing him in a casket and having men dump dirt into his grave jammed a big knot into my throat. I can still remember finding it hard to swallow. I got very quiet. And I never brought the subject up again.

Granddaddy died many years later. By then, I was a young man in the Marine Corps, stationed overseas on the island of Okinawa. Unable to attend his funeral, I took some time late one evening to sit near the ocean; I watched the seagulls playing near the surf, listened to the waves crashing against the shore, and cried my heart out. As the sun set into the sea, I remembered Granddaddy's words, and I told the Lord how grateful I was for His promise, that, when He returned, He would cause Granddaddy to "rise first," along with all the other saints, even before those who are alive are "caught up . . . to meet the Lord in the air."

Granddaddy would get his wish. The "full deal" would one day be his to enjoy.

Somehow, that helped relieve my grief, and I was comforted with the thought that the Lord, by taking that dear man of God in death, was giving him exactly what he had wanted. Granddaddy's own, personal full-load, death-and-all contract with God was being honored.

By the time the stars were beginning to shine, God had dried my tears. His Word had, once again, met a deep need in my life. Full of gratitude, I rose to my feet and, all alone on that distant beach—so far from home, yet so close to heaven—I lifted my hands to the heavens and at the top of my voice I shouted these words back to Him who gave them:

> But we do not want you to be uninformed, brethren, about those who are asleep, that you may not grieve, as do the rest who have no hope. For if we believe that Jesus died and rose again, even so God will bring with Him those who have fallen asleep in Jesus. For this we say to you by the word of the Lord, that we who are alive, and remain until the coming of the Lord, shall not precede those who have fallen asleep. For the Lord Himself will descend from heaven with a shout, with the voice of the archangel, and with the trumpet of God; and the dead in Christ shall rise first. Then we who are alive and remain shall be caught up together with them in the clouds to meet the Lord in the air, and thus we shall always be with the Lord. Therefore comfort one another with these words.
>
> 1 Thesslonians 4:13–18

What comfort those words brought me, even though I was eight thousand miles from my granddaddy's grave. They still do. Thanks to his confidence in God's promise, I no longer find the subject of death all that mysterious or scary. If it didn't frighten my granddaddy, why should it frighten me? Like him, I now find myself looking forward to experiencing the "full deal." If that is His plan for me, I'm ready.

God's plan for Elijah, however, was altogether different. Unlike my granddaddy's, his was a no-death contract.

WAITING FOR THE WHIRLWIND

What a journey Elijah had been on! Trained at Cherith, shaped and refined at Zarephath, used magnificently on Mount Carmel, powerfully anointed to stand before King Ahab on more than a few occasions, and finally given the companionship of his friend, Elisha, the old prophet had emerged as God's man of the hour. Heroic almost beyond belief, yet humble of heart, Elijah seemed to have reached the pinnacle of life's experiences. But now he was going to top them all: He was going to dodge death. The grim reaper's scythe would miss him altogether.

Missing death puts Elijah in the very rare category of "deathless departures." Only two in all the recorded history of time have exited earth without passing through the jaws of death. That's right: Only two people have been immediately ushered from this earth directly into the presence of God, as far as the sacred record is concerned. Enoch was the first (Genesis 5:21–24). Elijah was the second. The last to experience this kind of departure will be those believers who are alive on earth at the time of Christ's return. We do not know the date or the hour, but we do know this: Those who are alive when Christ comes for His own will bypass death. Paul writes of this with assurance in his first letter to the Corinthians:

> Behold, I tell you a mystery; we shall not all sleep, but we shall all be changed, in a moment, in the twinkling of an eye, at the last trumpet; for the trumpet will sound, and the dead will be raised imperishable, and we shall be changed. For this perishable must put on the imper-

ishable, and this mortal must put on immortality. But when this per-
ishable will have put on the imperishable, and this mortal will have
put on immortality, then will come about the saying that is written,
Death is swallowed up in victory.

1 Corinthians 15:51–54

The remarkable part of Elijah's story is that he *knew* he was going to be
taken up to heaven without dying. Because of this, he leaves us a fitting
example of how we should be living in anticipation of Christ's return.

From the context, it is obvious that God gave Elijah information about
his ultimate departure ahead of time, although we are never told when or
how He did this. God also, as we shall see, made it known to "the sons of
the prophets," as well as to Elisha, the old prophet's close friend and di-
vinely chosen successor.

And it came about when the LORD was about to take up Elijah by a
whirlwind to heaven, that Elijah went with Elisha from Gilgal.

2 Kings 2:1

We have come to Elijah's last day on earth, when he will go up in "a whirlwind." The Hebrew here can also be translated, "in a gust, in a windy moment." In some kind of sweeping movement, Elijah would be caught up,
and in that instant he would be gone from this earth into God's presence.

Now God had not only told Elijah that this would happen and how it
would happen, He also had told him where it would happen. This explains
why we see Elijah moving quickly toward the Jordan.

As you read the narrative, imagine the scene as it unfolds.

And Elijah said to Elisha, "Stay here please, for the LORD has sent me
as far as Bethel." But Elisha said, "As the LORD lives and as you yourself live, I will not leave you." So they went down to Bethel.

Then the sons of the prophets who were at Bethel came out to
Elisha and said to him, "Do you know that the LORD will take away
your master from over you today?" And he said, "Yes, I know; be still."

And Elijah said to him, "Elisha, please stay here, for the LORD has sent me to Jericho." But he said, "As the LORD lives, and as you yourself live, I will not leave you." So they came to Jericho.

And the sons of the prophets who were at Jericho approached Elisha and said to him, "Do you know that the LORD will take away your master from over you today?" And he answered, "Yes, I know; be still."

Then Elijah said to him, "Please stay here, for the LORD has sent me to the Jordan." And he said, "As the LORD lives, and as you yourself live, I will not leave you." So the two of them went on.

2 Kings 2:2–6

I am confident that God had told his humble and faithful prophet, "The Jordan will be the place of your departure." But if that was the case, why was Elijah wandering around the countryside, going to Gilgal, Bethel, and Jericho? Why not go straight to the Jordan?

Historians tell us that the schools of the prophets were located at Gilgal, Bethel, and Jericho. These were the early "seminaries," if you will, most likely founded by Samuel—schools where young men were trained to undertake the sacred calling and the disciplined lifestyle of a prophet. I believe that one reason for Elijah's unusual journey to the Jordan was his desire to meet one last time with the young prophets-in-training, "the sons of the prophets," and offer final words of encouragement to those who would carry the torch of truth after his departure.

Beyond that, however, was a deeper reason.

At both Bethel and Jericho, the sons of the prophets asked Elisha the same question: "Do you know that the Lord will take away your master from over you today?"

Both times Elisha gave the same answer: "Yes, I know. Now be quiet."

Yes, Elisha assured the sons of the prophets, this was the day Elijah would be taken. But why did he tell the young men to be quiet? I believe he did so because he did not want them to disturb Elijah with their questions and all the natural conversation and dialogue that would flow on the heels of the amazing information the aging prophet was sharing. Elisha knew that Elijah was lost in a unique time of reflection and needed peace and quiet.

How many times have you heard it said that when a person dies, his whole life passes in review before him? How do people know that? Wouldn't you have to die to know that? And when you die you are no longer around to tell anyone what it was like. Yet the truth is, those of us who have had close calls, close brushes with death—a terrible illness, an almost-drowning, a serious accident—have had the experience, haven't we? We've seen a great panorama, an instant mural of the past, flash before our eyes. Such a never-to-be-forgotten phenomenon makes us reflect, doesn't it? That, I believe, is what happened to Elijah.

Elisha, his close friend, the younger prophet to whom he would pass his mantle of authority, saw that he needed time to reflect on all that was happening. And so Elisha says, in effect, "No questions, please. You fellows, be quiet. Give Elijah room, let him think and reflect."

REFLECTION: PLACES OF MEANING

As I mentioned earlier, specific places in Scripture often have great significance. We have seen that already in our study of the life of Elijah. These last three places he visits are no exception.

Gilgal was *the place of beginning*. According to Joshua 4, Gilgal was where the children of Israel camped just after they crossed the Jordan into Canaan. If you remember your biblical history, you'll recall that this was the beginning point where they were still safe and secure, just before they began their invasion into enemy territory.

> Now the people came up from the Jordan on the tenth of the first month and camped at Gilgal on the eastern edge of Jericho.
>
> Joshua 4:19

At Gilgal the Israelites stood on the verge of battle, listening to Joshua, their commander-in-chief, give the final directions and strategy, which God had given him. They were near the place of battle but were not there yet.

They were still in the place of safety, the place of communion, the place of sharing, the place of preparation.

Gilgal was the place of beginning for Elijah's final journey.

Bethel, Elijah's next stop, *was the place of prayer.* "Beth-el" means "house of God." As explained earlier, it's where Abraham built an altar and where he often met with his Lord.

> Then he proceeded from there to the mountain on the east of Bethel, and pitched his tent, with Bethel on the west and Ai on the east; and there he built an altar to the LORD and called upon the name of the LORD.
>
> Genesis 12:8

During his times of searching and struggle, as well as times of dedication and preparation, the patriarch frequently returned to Bethel, the place where he had first worshiped and communed with God.

Possibly, when Elijah walked the streets of ancient Bethel, gazing at stones still marked with the etchings of his spiritual ancestors, he thought back upon all the altars of his own life. First, there was the altar at the brook Cherith, where he had to trust God against insuperable odds. He had little food. He had no shelter. He was a wanted man. Elijah's communion with God was never stronger than it was there at the altar by that quiet, flowing brook.

Elijah's next altar was at Zarephath where he stayed with the widow and her son who were about to starve to death. At that place, Elijah brought their daily needs before his God. It was there also that his faith matured to the point where he could, with confidence in the Lord, take the widow's dead son into his arms and breathe new life into his body. How could Elijah ever forget the victories won in prayer at the altar of Zarephath?

As he walked the streets of Bethel, Elijah saw the altars of his own life pass in review.

Elijah then went to *Jericho, the place of battle.* Jericho was the place where God's people had driven a formidable wedge into the opposition. Jericho was to the Hebrews what D-day was to the Americans in World

War II. It was Normandy for God's people. Jericho was a city of magnificent and vivid memories.

Elijah, in his mind's eye, saw the walls as they fell; he heard the swish of the arrows and the cry of the enemy. And in that moving place of battle, Elijah, no doubt, relived the battles of his own life.

At Mount Carmel he battled the evil forces of Baal. And we must not forget his numerous battles with Ahab and his wicked wife, Jezebel. Under the juniper tree Elijah had waged his own personal battle, where he had despaired of life.

Knowing it was his last day on earth, Elijah surely revisited and relived the battles of the past.

Finally, Elijah traveled on to the *Jordan,* which *was the place of death*— not just physical death, but death of the self-life. There, Elijah remembered those days when he had died to his own wishes, his own plans, and surrendered the strength of his own flesh. Through the passing years, this rugged, muscular, determined man of Tishbeh had learned to rely on his God, not himself. He had learned to walk in the strength of the Lord, not in his own will. He had learned to submit, to wait, to obey.

Such self-denial does not come naturally. It is a learned virtue, encouraged by few and modeled by even fewer, especially among those who are what we've come to know as Type A personalities. Prophets are notorious for exhibiting this temperament, which makes Elijah all the more remarkable. Without hedging in heroism, he was as soft clay in his Master's hands. As we saw earlier, he did his best work "under the shadow of the Almighty." His was a life of power, because he had come to the place where he welcomed the death of his own desires, if it meant the display of God's greater glory.

The place of beginning, the place of the prayer, the place of battle, the place of death. We, too, have such places in our lives.

APPLICATION: TIMES OF SEARCHING

First, there's a place of beginning. That's home base—the very beginning of our Christian experience when we are born anew. That is our place of a whole new beginning. At our own Gilgal, we become brand new.

For some of us, that place of beginning, that home base, is far in the past. Search back in your memory. Can you remember when you took your first few baby steps? You tottered a little, and those who loved and mentored you helped steady you on your feet. And you learned the basics of life: how to get into the Word; how to pray; how to have time with God; how to share your faith.

And then comes the place of prayer. Remember? You first began to learn what it was to sacrifice, to surrender things dear and precious to you. For some it was a miscarriage or the loss of a child. For some it was the loss of a husband or wife. Perhaps for you it was the loss of a job, or your own business, or a lifelong dream never to be realized. Coming all alone to your own Bethel, you learned to pray.

God did a real work in your life as He carried you from that place of communion to the next stage He planned for you. And because you'd learned the value of prayer, you built your altar, and you learned even more at His feet. Search back in time. Pause . . . remember?

Next, there is Jericho—the place of battle. Some of you have had serious battles in your life: battles with rebellion, battles with addictions, battles with your thought life, battles with doubt, battles with the flesh. You have endured difficult struggles at the Jericho of your life, haven't you?

And finally, there is the Jordan, the place of death. Some of you may be aware that you will soon be approaching this place, should the doctor's prognosis be accurate. Most of us, of course, don't know how soon we will reach our Jordan. It could be decades away . . . or as near as the next breath.

But there is also another kind of death, and that is the death of self, when we learn the necessity of self-denial. This death is part of "taking up His cross and following Him" (Matthew 10:38). When we *finally* learn to do that—and it is *such* a difficult rite of passage—peace pervades.

SEPARATION: WORDS OF DEPARTURE

Finally, Elijah reached the Jordan, his ultimate earthly destination, and Elisha said, "As the Lord lives, I will not leave you."

Elijah had been trying to separate himself from Elisha ever since Gilgal. I don't think he was so much trying to get rid of Elisha as he was putting his close companion, his successor-in-the-making, to the test. "Elisha, you may not want to go with me at Gilgal or at Bethel or at Jericho, certainly not the Jordan." But Elisha was relentless. He stayed by the old prophet's side.

There's an expression in football that is used when a player in the defensive backfield follows closely as a wide receiver runs a pattern to catch the pass. If the defensive back stays on the receiver the entire time, we say he is "in his shirt." The defensive player stays so close that the offensive receiver later shakes his head and mumbles, "The guy was in my shirt." That means, "He was glued to me. I couldn't shake him. He was right there, start to finish."

That's Elisha! He said to Elijah, "I'm in your shirt, my friend. You're not getting rid of me. I'm right here with you the whole time."

Remember how he said it?

> And he [Elisha] said, "As the LORD lives, and as you yourself live, I will not leave you." So the two of them went on.
>
> 2 Kings 2:6

We need a few Elishas in our lives, don't we? They bring us strength. And they are a rare breed indeed! They're our intimate friends. They are those who are there for us, with us, available to us—to hear us, to help us, to soften the blows of our critics, to support us in prayer, to stay in our corners, bringing us both encouragement and objectivity. (I know what I'm talking about here, having had a few of my own Elishas. As I look back, it is hard to imagine my life without them. I could not have gone on!)

When the two men stopped at the Jordan, the scene suddenly changed.

Read the story slowly. Again, let your mind run free as you imagine this unusual dialogue and miraculous event:

> Fifty men of the company of the prophets went and stood at a distance, facing the place where Elijah and Elisha had stopped at the Jordan. Elijah took his cloak, rolled it up and struck the water with it.

> The water divided to the right and to the left, and the two of them
> crossed over on dry ground.
>
> When they had crossed, Elijah said to Elisha, "Tell me, what can I
> do for you before I am taken from you?"
>
> "Let me inherit a double portion of your spirit," Elisha replied.
>
> "You have asked a difficult thing," Elijah said, "yet if you see me
> when I am taken from you, it will be yours—otherwise not."
>
> 2 Kings 2:7–10, NIV

This miracle is reminiscent of the one that occurred centuries earlier, when God miraculously parted the Red Sea, and Moses and the children of Israel walked across on dry ground. In this case, the waters of the Jordan parted, allowing Elijah and Elisha to cross the river on dry ground.

Then Elijah turns to his friend and asks, "What can I do for you before I go? Before the Lord takes me from this earth?"

Notice Elisha's immediate request. This is a man who thinks big, and he isn't hesitant to reveal it. He says, "Elijah, you've done some great miracles in your life. But I'd like to have a double dose of your spirit so I might know twice the power!" What a *grand* request!

Don't be afraid to ask big things of God. He says, "I want to give you a lot, you know. Ask for it!" Yet the mind-set of too many Christians is far too limited. We would do well to learn a lesson about vision from Elijah's faithful companion.

Yet even Elijah, with all the great things he's asked of God—remember, this is the man who called down fire from heaven—is a bit taken aback here. "That's a tough one," he tells Elisha. "But if you see me when I'm taken from you, then what you ask shall be yours. If you don't, it will not be."

You can believe Elisha determined at that moment never to let Elijah out of his sight. He would hardly blink again! But he didn't have long to wait and watch. Without further delay, it happened.

> As they were walking along and talking together, suddenly a chariot
> of fire and horses of fire appeared and separated the two of them, and
> Elijah went up to heaven in a whirlwind.
>
> 2 Kings 2:11, NIV

I love that! "They were walking along and talking together." Elijah was not preaching or prophesying. It was just the two intimate friends walking along together and talking. What a fantastic moment that must have been. And suddenly "a chariot of fire and horses of fire appeared, and Elijah went up to heaven in a whirlwind."

Just like that! Instantly he was gone "up to heaven in a whirlwind."

Elisha saw the chariots, and he cried out in amazement and awe. His heart must have been pounding in his throat, his eyes as big as saucers. His adrenaline must have surged, big time. Then, *whoosh!* The whirlwind blew hard against his robe and hair and beard, and Elijah was gone. Amazing moment!

CONSUMMATION: MANTLE OF POWER

Elisha saw this and cried out, "My father! My father! The chariots and horsemen of Israel!" And Elisha saw him no more. Then he took hold of his own clothes and tore them apart.

He picked up the cloak that had fallen from Elijah and went back and stood on the bank of the Jordan. Then he took the cloak that had fallen from him and struck the water with it. "Where now is the LORD, the God of Elijah?" he asked. When he struck the water, it divided to the right and to the left, and he crossed over.

The company of the prophets from Jericho, who were watching, said, "The spirit of Elijah is resting on Elisha." And they went to meet him and bowed to the ground before him.

2 Kings 2:12–15, NIV

Elijah's no-death contract suddenly went into effect.

Elijah, prophet of power . . . gone. Elisha, prophet of double power . . . here, ready, and about to be used greatly by his God.

When a man or woman of God dies, nothing of God dies. We tend to forget this. We get so caught up in the lives of certain individuals that we begin to think we cannot do without them. What limited thinking! When even a mighty servant is gone, God has seven thousand who have never bowed the knee to Baal. He has them ready, waiting in the wings. Classic case in point: Elisha. God always has a back-up plan.

Think about it. Down through the ages He has had His men and women in every era to carry on His work. Never once has God been frustrated, wondering, "What will My people do now that he's gone? Now that she's no longer with them?" Our Creator-God is omnipotent. He is never caught shorthanded.

Elisha may have been momentarily surprised and stunned, but that didn't last long. Remembering Elijah's words, he reached down and picked up the prophet's cloak. Claiming the power that now was his, he crossed back over the Jordan and began his own prophetic ministry from that time on. God's plan never missed a beat.

Exit Elijah. Enter Elisha.

We can't help but wonder if, in the years to come, Elisha didn't stop and study that old mantle, calling to mind those great days of the past when his mentor and friend stood alone, representing God's presence and proclaiming God's message. The memory of the older Elijah—a man of heroism and humility—served to strengthen the younger Elisha, whom God destined to use in even greater ways.

There are times, to this day, when I call to mind my granddaddy, L. O. Lundy. His wise words of counsel still linger. His life of quiet, deep character sometimes seems so close to me I can almost feel his warm breath on the back of my neck. Yes, to this day, I miss him, but the mantle of his memory spurs me on to greater heights and deeper devotion.

The good news is this: I will one day see him. And we, together, will worship the same Lord face to face, " . . . and thus we shall always be with the Lord."

CONCLUSION

Elijah: A Man of Heroism & Humility

The Christian's greatest goal is to be like Christ. We want to emulate His exemplary life, model His method of teaching, resist temptation as He resisted it, handle conflicts as He did, focus on the mission God calls us to accomplish as Christ focused on His. And certainly it is our desire to commune with the Father as the Son did throughout His ministry and suffering. No greater compliment can be given than this one: "When I am with that person, it's like I'm in the presence of Jesus Himself."

Throughout this study of Elijah, I have often thought of how closely the great prophet's life resembled the Messiah, who was yet to come: the way he spent time alone; the courage he showed as he stood in the presence of his enemy and delivered God's message; the power he exhibited when it took a miracle to convince his audience that he was a man with a message from God—the one true God; the compassion he demonstrated when he cared about the widow's grief and brought her son back to life; even the anguish he felt in his own Gethsemane as he wrestled in his soul. And finally, how much like Christ was his departure. As others stood staring, he was taken up to heaven out of their sight (Matthew 16:13–14).

Is it any surprise, then, that when our Savior asked His disciples, "Who do people say that the Son of Man is?" the answer from some was, "Elijah." Why, of course! Small wonder, for in many ways their lives paralleled. And when the two men appeared before Jesus and three of His disciples on the Mount of Transfiguration, one was Moses, and the other was none other than Elijah (Matthew 17:3).

Anyone making a list of the greatest men of the Bible—even a short list—would certainly include Elijah. Few others are better models of the two traits I have emphasized again and again throughout this book: heroism and humility. Whoever thinks of Christ solely as tenderness, benevolence, and patience, need only study Elijah. Like the prophet of Tishbeh, Jesus could speak scorching words of judgment and retribution. And lest anyone believe our Lord was always a man of powerful presence, working mighty miracles and taking a strong stand against the hypocrisy of the Pharisees, again, return to Elijah. See him in the quiet solitude of Cherith, in the refining months at Zarephath and the extended time he spent throughout his ministry in protracted prayer.

Studying Elijah offers us an opportunity to see unique glimpses of Jesus reflected in the prophet's life, as we await that moment when we shall see Him face to face in all His glory. To be completely candid with you, as I came toward the end of the last chapter, I found myself longing for my eternal home. I felt the pull of heaven on my heart, and I was strangely envious of Elijah's being taken up by a whirlwind into the very presence of God. Anytime the Lord's ready to take me, let me say again, I'm ready to go!

Years ago, a book of devotional verse entitled *Immanuel's Land and Other Pieces* was published by someone known simply as A. R. C. We now know the author was Anne Ross Cousin, but because she wanted all the glory of that publication to go to her Lord, she chose to use only her initials.

One of the compositions in this quaint volume is "In Immanuel's Land." In this piece, which became a great old hymn of the faith, Anne Ross Cousin offers a clear definition of our eternal home: It is not *our* land but Immanuel's land. We are such this-world-only dwellers, so rooted and earthbound in our current day and age. But a hymn like this helps to sweep away the debris and trash of the temporal and reveals the timeless relevance and reality of the eternal.

The first and final stanzas say it all:

> The sands of time are sinking,
> The dawn of heaven breaks;
> The summer morn I've sighed for,
> The fair, sweet morn awakes:
> Dark, dark hath been the midnight,
> But dayspring is at hand,
> And glory, glory dwelleth
> In Immanuel's land.

> The Bride eyes not her garment,
> But her dear Bridegroom's face;
> I will not gaze at glory
> But on my King of grace.
> Not at the crown He giveth
> But on His pierced hand,
> The Lamb is all the glory
> Of Immanuel's land.[1]

Elijah's heroic and humble life urges us to be like Christ—to lift our eyes from the grit and grind of today's woes and to turn our attention to the glory and hope of another land. Immanuel's land! And in that frame of mind, we'll redirect our gaze from who gets the glory to who gives the grace.

And then, while fully focused on Him—our King of grace, the Lamb—the deepest longings of our souls will be satisfied.

Endnotes

Elijah: A Man of Heroism & Humility

INTRODUCTION

1 . J. Steven Wilkins, *Call of Duty: The Sterling Nobility of Robert E. Lee* (Nashville, Tenn.: Cumberland House Publishing, 1997), 225.

CHAPTER ONE

1 Merrill F. Unger, *Unger's Bible Dictionary* (Chicago, Ill.: The Moody Bible Institute of Chicago, 1957; rev. ed. 1988), 1290.

2. J. Oswald Sanders, *Robust in Faith* (Chicago: Ill.: Moody Press, 1965), 125–126.

2. Harry Emerson Fosdick, *Great Voices of the Reformation* (New York: Random House, Inc., 1952), 242.

CHAPTER TWO

1. A. W. Tozer, *The Root of the Righteous* (Harrisburg, PA.: Christian Publications, Inc., 1955), 137.

2. Arthur W. Pink, *The Life of Elijah* (Grand Rapids, Mich.: Zondervan Publishing House, 1956), 41.

3. Douglas Southall Freeman, *R. E. Lee* (New York: Charles Scribner's Sons, 1947), 3:216.

4. F. B. Meyer, *Elijah: And the Secret of His Power* (London: Morgan & Scott, n.d.), 21.

5. E. May Grimes, "Speak, Lord, in the Stillness," first stanza, n.d.

6. Vance Havner, *It Is Toward Evening* (Westwood, N.J.: Fleming H. Revell Company, 1968), 39–40.

7. William M. Elliott, Jr. *For the Living of These Days,* as quoted by Richard H. Seume in *Shoes for the Road* (Chicago, Ill.: Moody Bible Institute, 1974), 42.

8. Ella Wheeler Wilcox, "Gethsemane," from *Poems of Power* W. B. Conkey Company, Publishers, n.d.).

CHAPTER THREE

1. George Keith, "How Firm a Foundation," third stanza, n.d.

2. Arthur T. Pierson, *The Bible and Spiritual Life* (New York: Gospel Publishing, n.d.), 377.

3. "How Firm a Foundation."

CHAPTER FOUR

1. Source unknown.

2. V. Raymond Edman, *In Quietness and Confidence* (Wheaton, Ill.: Scripture Press, 1956), 63.

CHAPTER FIVE

1. Alfred Edersheim, *Bible History: Old Testament* (Grand Rapids, Mich.: William R. Eerdmans Publishing Company, n.d.), 17–18.

CHAPTER SIX

1. Bernard Ramm, *Protestant Biblical Interpretation* (Grand Rapids, Mich.: Baker Book House, 1970), 194.
2. "2 Holiness Preachers Die in a Test of Faith," *Los Angeles Times,* April 10, 1973, sec. I, p. 14.

CHAPTER SEVEN

1. C. H. Spurgeon, *Lectures to My Students* (Grand Rapids, Mich.: Zondervan Publishing House, 1954), 158–162.

CHAPTER EIGHT

1. A. W. Tozer, *The Knowledge of the Holy* (New York: Harper and Brothers Publishers, 1961), 94–95.

CHAPTER NINE

1. J. Oswald Sanders, *Spiritual Leadership* (Chicago, Ill.: Moody Press, 1967, 1980), 169.
2. James Burns, *Revivals, Their Laws and Leaders* (London: Hodder & Stoughton, 1909), 167–68.
3. Amy Carmichael, "God, harden me . . ." © The Dohnavur Fellowship, n.d.

CONCLUSION

1. Anne Ross Cousin, "The Sands of Time Are Sinking," first and fourth stanzas, n.d.

ADDITIONAL SELECTIONS FROM
THE GREAT LIVES SERIES

GREAT LIVES SERIES: VOLUME 1
DAVID

This first volume in the "Great Lives" series masterfully takes readers on an unforgettable journey through the life of a humble shepherd boy whom God transforms into a king tempered with courage and grace. A national bestseller.

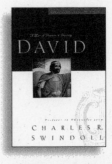

GREAT LIVES SERIES: VOLUME 2
ESTHER

Volume 2 of Charles Swindoll's "Great Lives" series, *Esther* is the passionate story of one woman's courageous struggle to save her people from certain destruction. Using the life of Esther, Swindoll explains the power of divine providence.

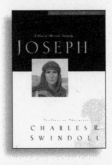

GREAT LIVES SERIES: VOLUME 3
JOSEPH

The third volume in Charles Swindoll's epic "Great Lives" series presents Joseph—and the circumstances that shaped him—as never before. This fresh look at one of the most intriguing characters in the Old Testament focuses on the virtue of forgiveness in the face of deceit and betrayal.

GREAT LIVES SERIES: VOLUME 4
MOSES

Meet the real Moses—not a Hollywood version—in this fascinating personality profile from God's Word. Swindoll reveals the drama and details of Moses' life while applying the lessons learned to our own daily dilemmas.

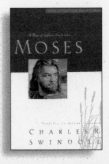

DROPPING YOUR GUARD

Charles Swindoll unveils a biblical blueprint for rich relationships in this life-changing classic. In this updated version of his best-selling book, Swindoll poignantly and honestly portrays the need for authentic love and transparency.

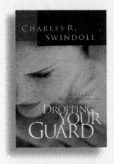

FINISHING TOUCH, THE

When the going gets tough, most people just quit. This daily devotional challenges us to persevere and to finish well the race set before us as God finishes in us the good work He began. This popular volume is Swindoll's first collection of daily readings.

FLYING CLOSER TO THE FLAME

Best-selling author Charles Swindoll explores the void that exists in many Christian's lives due to a lack of understanding about the Holy Spirit. In *Flying Closer to the Flame,* he challenges readers toward a deeper, more intimate relationship with the Holy Spirit.

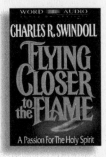

GRACE AWAKENING, THE

In this best-selling classic, Charles Swindoll awakens readers to the life-impacting realities of God's grace, the freedom and joy it brings, the fear it cures, the strength it lends to relationships, and the ever-increasing desire to know God. A modern-day classic from Charles Swindoll.

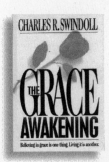

GROWING UP IN GOD'S FAMILY

Growing older doesn't necessarily mean growing up or maturing in Christ. Using the stages of physical growth—birth and infancy, childhood, adolescence, and adulthood—to describe the phases of spiritual maturity, Swindoll encourages Christians to pursue spiritual growth.

HAND ME ANOTHER BRICK

Most of us could benefit from wise advice on how to be a more effective leader at work and at home. Charles Swindoll delves deep into the life of Nehemiah to show how to handle the issues of motivation, discouragement, and adversity with integrity.

HOPE AGAIN

Combining the New Testament teachings of Peter and the insights of one of the most popular authors of our day, *Hope Again* is an encouraging, enlivening, and refreshing look at why we can dare to hope no matter who we are, no matter what we face.

IMPROVING YOUR SERVE

In this classic volume, Charles Swindoll uniquely shows the important aspects of authentic servanthood, such as: What it takes to serve unselfishly, why a servant has such a powerful influence, and what challenges and rewards a servant can expect.

LAUGH AGAIN

Discover outrageous joy in this modern classic. Charles Swindoll shows how we can live in the present, say "no" to negativism, and realize that while no one's life is perfect, joy is always available. Applying scriptural truths in a practical way, Swindoll shows readers how to laugh again.

LIVING ABOVE THE LEVEL OF MEDIOCRITY

Charles Swindoll tackles the problem of mediocrity in one of his most popular books. With his trademark stories and practical insight, he boldly confronts the issues of self-discipline, laziness, and our tendency to accept less than what we deserve, drawing clear lines between the pursuit of excellence and the pursuit of success in the eyes of the world.

LIVING ON THE RAGGED EDGE

Here is an intimate glimpse into Solomon's ancient journal, Ecclesiastes, in which the young king's desperate quest for satisfaction—in work, in sexual conquest, in all the trappings afforded by his fabulous wealth—was as futile as trying to "catch the wind." For those struggling with the anxieties and frustrations of our modern era, the good news is that you can find perspective and joy amid the struggle.

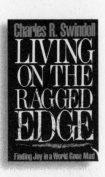

ROAD TO ARMAGEDDON, THE
Various Authors

The end of a century. A new millennium. For Christians everywhere, there is little doubt that these are the last days, as we move down the road to Armageddon. This book features six of the most respected scholars and teachers on Bible prophecy and coming world events. An important tool for understanding the future.

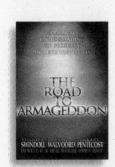

SIMPLE FAITH

Must we run at a pace between maddening and insane to prove we're among the faithful? Is this really how the Prince of Peace would have us live? In this book, Swindoll answers with a resounding, "No!," showing how Christians can break free from exhausting, performance-based faith, back to the simplicity of the Sermon on the Mount.

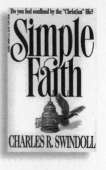

START WHERE YOU ARE

"To start fresh, to start over, to start anything, you have to know where you are," says Charles Swindoll. "Seldom does anybody just happen to end up on a right road." In *Start Where You Are*, Swindoll offers upbeat and practical advice on creating a life worth living, no matter what the circumstances are now or where they may lead in the future.

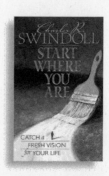

STRENGTHENING YOUR GRIP

As only he can, Charles Swindoll combines biblical insights with unforgettable stories that inspire readers to strengthen their spiritual grip on issues such as family, prayer, integrity, and purity.

SUDDENLY ONE MORNING

Through the eyes of a shopkeeper on the main street of Jerusalem, readers experience the life-changing events of a week that begins with a parade and ends with an empty grave. This Easter gift book combines an original Swindoll story with beautiful full-color art.

TALE OF THE TARDY OX CART, THE

In *The Tale of The Tardy Ox Cart*, Charles Swindoll shares from his life-long collection of his and others' personal stories, sermons, and anecdotes. 1501 various illustrations are arranged by subjects alphabetically for quick and easy access. A perfect resource for all pastors and preachers.

THREE STEPS FORWARDS, TWO STEPS BACK

Charles Swindoll reminds readers that our problems are not solved by simple answers or all-too-easy clichés. Instead, he offers practical ways to walk with God through the realities of life—including times of fear, stress, anger, and temptation.

YOU AND YOUR CHILD

Best-selling author and veteran parent and grandparent Charles Swindoll believes that the key to successful parenting lies in becoming a "student" of your children—learning the distinct bent and blueprint of each child. Here's practical advice for parents wishing to launch confident, capable young adults in today's ever-changing world.